MUSINGS OF A WALMART GREETER

MUSINGS OF A WALMART GREETER

ENTERTAINING AND INSPIRING STORIES THAT COULD ONLY HAPPEN IN THE GREATEST RETAIL STORE ON EARTH

GARRY WARNER

Acclaim Press
MORLEY, MISSOURI

Acclaim Press
Your Next Great Book

P.O. Box 238
Morley, MO 63767
(573) 472-9800
www.acclaimpress.com

Book Design: Frene Melton
Cover Design: Rodney Atchley
Cover photo by Daniel Byrd

Copyright © 2024, Garry Warner
All Rights Reserved.

No part of this book shall be reproduced or transmitted in any form or by any means, electronic or mechanical, including photocopying, recording or by an information or retrieval system, except in the case of brief quotations embodied in articles and reviews, without the prior written consent of the publisher. The scanning, uploading, and distribution of this book via the Internet or via any other means without permission of the publisher is illegal and punishable by law.

ISBN: 978-1-956027-96-9 | 1-956027-96-3
Library of Congress Control Number: 2024942986

First Printing: 2024
Printed in the United States of America
10 9 8 7 6 5 4 3 2 1

This publication was produced using available information.
The publisher regrets it cannot assume responsibility for errors or omissions.

Contents

Acknowledgments................................... 6
Me!... 11
Iwo Jima.. 22
The Day Sam Came to Town 26
Those Electric Carts!............................. 29
Thou Shalt Not Steal.............................. 34
Those Amazing Associates!......................... 40
Birthdays... 47
Obesity... 50
Those Sagging Pants!.............................. 54
The Devil Made Me Do It!.......................... 58
Sherita... 63
Those Service Animals............................. 68
The Bird Lady..................................... 74
Wanda... 76
The Man With No Pants!............................ 80
Wally... 84
The Covid Calamity................................ 90
Till Death Do Us Part............................. 95
Those Carts!...................................... 104
Leggings and Pajamas.............................. 111
Donald.. 115
Special Needs and Disabilities.................... 119
Store Number 9.................................... 125
Let Freedom Ring.................................. 135
God And Me.. 141
Walmart Facts..................................... 148
About the Author.................................. 151
Index... 152

Acknowledgments

Books don't just happen. Authors need support. They need inspiration, and they need encouragement. This book is no exception. There are many people that have lifted and guided me through this seven-year adventure.

My beloved Shirley, you were the first! Your love and devotion for thirty-nine beautiful years, and your amazing faith gave me strength and determination every day this past seven years to finish this book. The authors should be Garry AND Shirley Warner!

This book would never have happened if my family doctor, Dr. Cully Bryant, had not encouraged me to start a journal after Shirley's death. He is not only my doctor, but he is also a good friend from church. I was dealing with severe depression after her death, and my church family was surrounding me with lots of support. Cully is also a published author, and he suggested journaling.

Although neither of us knew it, "Musings of a Walmart Greeter" was probably born that day! Thank you, Cully! You not only treated my infirmities. You provided medicine for my soul!

My family has been a HUGE support on this journey. My stepdaughter, Sheri, and my four stepchildren in the Philippines, Joy, Jerry, Jai, Jeff, all encouraged me along the way. When I was trying to rebuild my life after my second wife's death in 2021, and later after I went through seven surgeries in six months, they surrounded me with love.

There was also love and encouragement from my nieces, Judy and Rita, and Cathy, my cousin. Thank you! THANK YOU! I love all of you!

My greatest fan and most amazing encourager and critic has been my good friend and coffee buddy, Louis Watkins. Louis has pored over every word in "Musings". When I was ready to give up after my precious Nelia had her stroke and then died, he gently kept me going. He was there again a year later when I had all those surgeries. His couch has provided me a place to retreat, to regroup, to laugh, and cry. He has been a great friend through it all! Thank you, Louis! Your friendship is a true blessing!

There are some that didn't make it to the publishing. My sister, Patty, and my sister-in-law, Betty, who was really just like a sister, both went on to their eternal reward during the writing of this book. They were always calling or messaging me about some of the stories. I love you and miss you!

My high school classmate and college roommate, Terry, asked me about the book every time we talked. You died way too soon, good friend!

There are so many other friends and family that were there to encourage me along the way, but my greatest appreciation goes to all the customers and Walmart associates I have met while writing "Musings". You were the stories! You were the inspirations! You were the reasons this book HAD to be written!

Thank you! Thank you!! THANK YOU!!!

Special thanks to Daniel Byrd for the picture gracing my book cover. Your photography always excels, and this picture was no exception!

Finally, I give thanks to God. I have written a lot about my faith in this book. Every detail in this book has been discussed with my Lord Jesus. We have talked and prayed over every story. We have been together in the valleys. We have been together on the mountaintops! I hope I have lived up to His Heavenly expectations. Any credit goes to Him! To God goes the glory!!!

To my readers, I hope you will enjoy the ride. I hope it will make you smile. I hope you will laugh out loud. I hope it will make you cry. I hope it will make you proud. I hope you will look upon Walmart a little differently. I hope it will make you think. I hope you will feel my faith, and how God has touched my life and sustained me. I hope you examine YOUR story! You matter!

Enjoy!

MUSINGS OF A WALMART GREETER

ENTERTAINING AND INSPIRING STORIES THAT COULD ONLY HAPPEN IN THE GREATEST RETAIL STORE ON EARTH

Me!

I suppose this book was always inevitable. I have spent my entire life with a fascination about people! We are an amazing lot! We can be creative. We can be funny. We can be disgusting. We can be disappointing. But one thing is constant…we are ALWAYS interesting! For forty-plus years I managed or owned auto dealerships, overseeing the sale of over 50,000 cars and trucks. I had a box seat to observe the best and worst of the human race. But NOTHING compared to my experience as a greeter at Walmart. Walmart is a microcosm of America.

On a daily basis, a cross section of our country comes through her doors. It is safe to say that I have seen just about everything in my time at the front door of the world's biggest retailer. I love my job! It's the worst paying job I have ever had, and the most rewarding! I get hugs every day! I get the opportunity to greet hundreds of forgotten lonely people, whose only social experience is a visit to our store. We turn their frowns upside down! When I see a really beautiful smile, I always encourage them to take it outside and change the world! Walmart has broad employment standards. They give opportunities to many people that other companies would never hire…and many become loyal hardworking associates. I work beside other senior citizens, and people with physical or mental disabilities. I work beside single parents struggling to make ends meet. I work beside people with all kinds of tattoos and piercings. I have seen every color in the rainbow in hair. Some are old…some are young…lots in between. They ALL have stories!

My story began eighty-one years ago on a farm in far western Kansas. I was born in 1943. The world was at war, and my parents were deeply affected like everyone living in those times. If you had met them, you would have wondered how they possibly could have married. Dad was the product of coarse blue collar parents that ruled with a paddle and an iron hand! Mother's parents came from a German Mennonite heritage, and raised their children with soft words and prayer. I grew up in that paradox! I was fascinated by the differences in others by the time I started school.

Life was hard back then. The war had caused shortages of about everything. Dad had been badly injured in a work accident about ten years before I was born while working in the Oregon woods during the Depression. A log had fallen on him, and broke over a hundred bones in his body. He had spent over a year in the hospital, and was affected by his injuries the rest of his life. He was not physically fit to fight in the war. He and my mother returned to Kansas after his injury, and they were able to buy their farm the year I was born. That farm in southwest Kearny county, Kansas would be their home almost the rest of their lives. My older brother and sister and my younger brother and I would all grow up there.

EVERYONE worked! My younger brother and I herded the cows in for milking every day. We gathered eggs in the chicken house. You have not LIVED until you have been attacked by an angry hen when you try to retrieve the egg she is sitting on! I hated those chickens! Mom had a HUGE garden! We worked every day in the summer weeding and watering that garden. We grew about everything. We ate fresh vegetables and some fruits, and mother canned and froze everything we did not eat. We always had cows and hogs. When the rains didn't come and we had a bad crop year, the cows and hogs got us through the tough times! I never NEEDED anything growing up! I WANTED lots of things I couldn't have. I wore clothes that mother had made or that were purchased from Montgomery Wards, Spiegel, or Sears Roebuck. My brother and I spent hours turning the pages of their catalogs! That's where I learned to dream! They were our "wish" books!

I drove my first farm tractor when I was nine years old. There was no power steering back then…no tractor cabs…no comfortable padded seats, and you turned a tractor in the field by using the left or right foot brake as you turned the steering wheel. I wasn't strong enough to turn the steering wheel, so I would stand on the brake with both feet and twist the steering wheel with both hands, and then spin it back so the plow would stay straight and not miss any untilled ground. Looking back, it was probably unsafe, and we would probably be breaking all kinds of laws today, but I was just one of MANY kids doing those kinds of things. Parents weren't thinking of breaking laws. We were just families living and worshiping and working together to make ends meet and finish the year getting a little further down the economic road.

There was still time for that big trip to town on Saturday with mother…dad rarely had time to join us… the trip to the drug store and a vanilla coke…the Saturday movie matinee…Roy Rogers…Gene Autry…Hopalong Cassidy, The Lone Ranger. There was 4H and Sunday School on Sundays. During the school year, my brother and I usually walked the 1 1/4 miles to the little one-room schoolhouse for school. I was 8th grade valedictorian…only one in my class! (Smile)! At night, we listened to all kinds of good programs on the radio for the entire family. That was after the third BIG meal mom had prepared that day! She was an amazing cook…almost all home grown, homemade, and REALLY good. There was no television. Mom saw to it that my brother and I read lots of books. I still do that today. Life was simple…and hard…and good!

All of us have special talents. I started singing solos while I was still in grade school. I sang in several special ensembles in high school, and lots more solos. By my senior year, I was being encouraged to pursue a career in music. My dad thought that was the stupidest idea he had ever heard, and mom thought I would be the next Frank Sinatra! Mom won, and I ended up at Bethany College in Lindsborg, Kansas. It was a small Lutheran liberal arts college with an outstanding music program. Bethany had a deep Swedish heritage. Almost everyone had a last name of Swenson, or Swanson, or Hanson, or Anderson, or Erickson, or, you get the idea!

The king of Sweden made several trips to visit. Every other year, the small town of 3,000 with five independent art galleries would explode in size as thousands of people descended to taste its rich heritage. The Terrible Swedes would take the field for the big homecoming celebration! Blue and Gold dominated the Kansas plains!

It was at Bethany that I got one of my early life lessons about choice. I was a pretty good athlete in addition to being an above average singer. I had run the quarter mile in high school, and we were participating in the fall intramural games. I was representing my fraternity in the 100 yard and 220 yard dashes and the quarter mile, and anchored the mile relay. I won all three of my individual races, and we won the relay as well. My running caught the attention of the track coach, and he invited me to join the track team.

The second week of practices, I was running practice laps. I looked up straight into the face of my voice professor and faculty advisor. He was 6 ft. 6 in. tall and weighed almost 300 pounds, so he had my attention! He asked me what I was doing. When I got through explaining with a little special emphasis on my running talents, he just shrugged and told me to choose between being an athlete or pursuing my music career. He would not allow me to do both. He told me I had a chance to become a really good singer with hard work. I had until the next morning to give him my answer. I turned in my track gear that night and finished the shortest track career in Bethany history.

It made me really angry and bitter at the time, but he was right. I would have been mediocre, and focusing on my voice was the right choice.

I attended Bethany for two years, and then transferred to Kansas State Teachers College (now Emporia State University) where I wrapped up my college years. A state university was a much less expensive place to finish my education. My voice professor was a cocky little tenor who had just returned from Europe where he sang professionally for several opera houses. He was very good as a performer and as a teacher. My senior year, he got me an audition with the New York Metropolitan Opera.

In my final semester before I would student teach and then graduate, I was dealt another one of those life experiences that change lives. I was in the final weeks of one of my required courses when I was called into the teaching professor's office after class. He proceeded to berate me as a student, and threatened to flunk me. There was a possible solution. I passed! I was not a homosexual.

I withdrew from his class, and took an incomplete to avoid an "F" on my transcript. The dean backed the professor, so I finished the semester, then dropped out of college. The Vietnam War was raging, and young men were being called in for physicals, and sent off to basic training.

Rather than let that happen, I auditioned for the Air Force Singing Sergeants, and immediately was accepted. The plan was for me to take the Army physical since I had already received my draft notice. The Air Force would accept the Army physical, and I would be traveling around the world singing in three months.

Alas, that would not happen. Young men were walking into the building where the Army was conducting physicals carrying x-rays, doctor's excuses and letters from back home, and told in a few hours to get their affairs in order and report for duty. I couldn't wait to get out of there and enlist in the Air Force, and I flunked my physical!!!

When I was a junior in high school, I messed up a few vertebrae in my back helping Dad put a wheel weight on one of the farm tractors. Our hometown doctor put me in a brace for six months, and that brace finished my Air Force career before it started.

I was devastated! The Singing Sergeants were going to be my meal ticket to four great years of performing around the world and then launch a professional music career. Instead, a worthless professor and a stupid back injury had blown everything!

When you just turned twenty-three, and the wheels have come off your world, what do you do? Mom and Dad said come home for the summer, and regroup, and we would come up with a plan for the fall.

Wichita State University seemed like a good option. It would probably take an extra year, but I would still end up with my degree. We could figure out later whether a professional music career was in the cards.

Enrollment was to begin on August 28th. Classes would begin the next week. The summer had been a time to settle down and get my wits and confidence back. One of my college buddies was now living in Wichita, and we were going to share an apartment. I was ready to begin my new life.

August 25th began like every other hot summer day. I took time off from work that afternoon to get a haircut. My barber was putting the finishing touches on his good work when I looked up to see Dad walking into the barber shop.

He was biting his lower lip. It was not normal for him to be in town in the middle of the day unless he was making a parts run for some piece of farm equipment. Then I saw the tears, and knew something bad had happened. He couldn't talk, and I was sure something had happened to Mom.

It wasn't Mom, and it was bad. An Air Force chaplain and officer had just left the farm a few hours earlier to tell my parents their youngest son, my little brother, had died the day before of natural causes while serving in Southeast Asia. He had suffered a cerebral hemorrhage and died at age twenty-one. Larry wasn't just my little brother. He was my best friend. He was my confidant. We had been inseparable growing up. He was gone. If the wheels had jumped the track that last spring, the whole train exploded there in that barber shop. There would be no new college the next week. There would be nothing. Instead, a hard-working and God fearing family would prepare for their son's/sibling's last trip home.

It hit the town and surrounding communities like a bomb. He wouldn't get home until the early morning of September 5th. The funeral would be the next day. In the meantime, the world just came to a halt. We all faced that time in different ways. Dad was a total basket case. My brother and sister were brokenhearted. Mom was calm, and a pillar of Spiritual strength to our family and the community as well. I was brokenhearted and hurt and angry. I cursed God! I took long walks in the pasture beyond the farmstead, and yelled at Him for destroying our family! It was an exclamation point on the worst year of my life! Each time, Mother would be there when I returned, hugging me, gently consoling me and everyone else as we all struggled to understand why bad things happen to good people.

Cars and trucks kept coming all day and into the night. The next day, it would all start again. Every kind of covered dish and entree and dessert was stacked everywhere in the kitchen. Twenty-one farmer neighbors showed up with their tractors and wheat drills, and planted an entire crop in half a day. The phone never stopped ringing. Friends and relatives from all over the country were planning to be at the services.

Those days became a blur. Finally, August 5th arrived. Dad and I got up before dawn to drive the thirty miles to Syracuse, Kansas, where we would meet the train bringing Larry home. It was a beautiful, sunny morning. Long before we saw the train, we heard the mournful whistle sound. Then, there it was on the horizon, starting to slow down as it approached the small Western Kansas town. The only people at the depot were Dad and me, Chuck McFaddon, the local funeral director, and the station manager. The funeral coach was parked behind where we were standing with the rear door open.

As the long train slowly rolled to a stop, the station manager opened the sliding door of one of the rail cars, and Chuck and two train employees helped him slide a large wooden crate onto a freight cart. A young Air Force Sergeant stepped from one of the passenger cars, and walked toward us. Passenger's faces were pressed against windows just watching the whole spectacle unfold. Dad and I were just trying our best to keep emotions in check, and it was hard. He introduced himself to us, and then walked to the cart holding Larry's earthly body. As the men grabbed the cart tongue and began pulling and pushing it to the hearse, the young airman walked slowly beside the procession. When they began to slide the crate into the hearse, he slowly raised his right hand in a salute, and held it till the hearse door was closed. Then he took his place in the front seat beside Chuck, and they slowly drove away from the train station. Dad and I climbed back into the car to get ready for the funeral the next day.

September 6th dawned, and everyone could see that God had provided a beautiful Western Kansas late summer day for Larry's service. The Air Force Honor Guard from Colorado Springs arrived shortly after 8:00 a.m. They joined the young soldier that had been beside Larry's casket every public moment since he arrived in Syracuse. The entourage made the short trip from the funeral home to the First Christian Church across from the high school. After Chuck parked in front of the church, the honor guard took their places behind the coach, and lifted Larry, and carried him into the church.

Nobody had seen such a spectacle since World War II. School had already started, and administrators were allowing the students to silently watch. Residents had parked near the church, and stood at attention with hats off and heads bowed as Larry's casket was carried into the church. Our family followed the honor guard, and the church doors were closed. We would spend our last private moments that day saying our goodbyes. There were over one hundred family members from all over the country in attendance. They came from both coasts. They came from Texas and Oklahoma. They came from Arkansas and Tennessee. They sat in silence as each member took their turn beside the casket that would be closed for the service. Mother stood beside the casket, and comforted each one as they said their tearful goodbyes. Her courage and faith that day became a beacon to me that I still carry today. This was a woman that KNEW God, and God knew HER! I will NEVER forget her strength that came from the Lord!

We took turns standing with her, but she never wavered. After the family had taken their turns, Dad and Mom and my older brother, Bud, and sister Patty all joined together around the casket for the last time. The honor guard stood over at the side at attention, and Larry's escort saluted and held it. When we were through, Chuck and Jerry McFaddon stepped forward and closed the casket for the last time. The Stars and Stripes was placed over the casket, and the family adjourned to the church basement for a huge meal that had been prepared by the church ladies. The honor guard joined us, and then went upstairs to relieve Larry's escort, so he could eat. Larry was never left alone the entire time.

The funeral service was beautiful, Bob Osburne, a former pastor and close family friend, had been flown in to conduct the service. Mike Martinie, a college classmate, sang the Air Force hymn and provided the special music. The one hundred-plus family members were brought up from the church basement and around the side and reentered through the front door into the sanctuary where a large seating area had been reserved. As we walked, we passed by several hundred people who could not get inside the church. Every seat was filled. People were standing two and three deep around the sides and back of the sanctuary. There was no air conditioning, and the church windows had been opened for ventilation. Chairs and speakers were hurriedly set up in the church basement and outside, and the service began.

It was over in about an hour, and the Honor Guard commander quietly stood, and began softly barking orders. The young airmen stepped to the casket and carried it in a slow precise cadence to the waiting funeral coach. The door was closed, and Larry was ready for the journey to his final resting place.

The Hamilton County cemetery sits on a small hill about 2 1/2 miles Northwest of town. I remember getting out of the family car behind the hearse when we got to the cemetery, and looking back into town. The funeral procession could still be seen crawling slowly to join us. I found out later that over 500 people signed the funeral guest book. There were many in the crowd that didn't. School had been dismissed. Most businesses had closed for the day or for the funeral. Most came to the cemetery. Some came for the spectacle of a military funeral. Most came because they knew our family, or just wanted to show their support.

The graveside service was brief. The flag was folded, and presented to Mom. The command was given for the 21-gun salute, and the rifles were lifted and fired. As each volley exploded, my father jumped. I remember getting out of my chair and kneeling in front of him just holding his hand. He never really ever recovered from that loss. We would bury him in the same family plot twelve years later.

As I sat beside that casket in a little country cemetery in the middle of America that hot late summer day, I made a vow to my brother that would shape my life the next thirty-seven years. He had been cheated out of life. I promised him that I would accomplish TWICE as much with my life to compensate for his!

It turned out that there would be a brief pause before that promise would be kept. A few months later, I moved to Wichita, Kansas, and left Western Kansas for the last time. Those roots and values would stay with me to today, but right then, I was just bitter and torn and lost.

But God has a way of rescuing the drifters. Mom never gave up on me, and that promise made at the cemetery was gnawing at my soul. After a brief stint as a funeral attendant at a Wichita mortuary, and a very short at trying to sell life insurance, I landed a job working as a loan officer with a consumer finance company. I was on my way.

In 1969, I met my future wife. That story is in another chapter. In 1973, a friend referred me to Davis Moore Oldsmobile AMC. They offered me a job as finance manager, and my career in automotive sales that spanned 4 1/2 decades was off and running.

In 1977, Grant Davis backed his general manager, Sam Reagan, in buying a down and out Buick Dealership in Omaha, Nebraska. They tapped me to be the new car sales manager. Over the next nine years, we took that dealership from 250 cars sales a year to the number eight Buick dealership in the United States. There were lots of stories along the way, but they will have to be saved for another book. The demon in my promise to my brother was hard at work. I was a driven man!

In October, 1986, with the help of Grant and Sam, I became the minority partner in my own dealership in suburban St. Louis, Missouri. It was called Warner Pontiac GMC and later Oldsmobile. The store was located in a blighted part of the city. The décor was shabby and outdated, and the company was on the verge of bankruptcy when we bought it. But the price was cheap, and the dealership was mine!

We painted and washed and hired and fired. We sold and traded! Fifteen hour days were common, but we were making solid progress. Over the next few years, we built the franchise into a Pontiac Master Dealership which placed sales in the top ten percent in the country. We had the highest customer satisfaction index in the entire Pontiac family.

However, trouble was brewing. Warner Pontiac was in the middle of a declining part of St. Louis. It was becoming obvious that we need to be looking for a new and better location. That opportunity arose when General Motors approached me about Pontiac Buick GMC Mazda dealership in St. Peters. It was located in the fastest growing county in Missouri. At the last minute, one of my partners backed out, and the deal fell through.

A few weeks later, I was forced out as a minority partner, and at age 49, was starting over. This time, it would be completely by myself with only the support of my wife and many people who believed in me, even when I was having trouble believing in myself.

I remember that morning when The Oldsmobile Zone Manager called, and asked if I would be interested in going to Sikeston, Missouri to work with a General Motors dealership that needed some help. That was the summer of 1992, and here I still am, thirty-two years later.

So much has happened in those thirty-two years, opening and managing my premium used car store with Shirley, my first wife. I would lose her in 2010 and close my business. I would marry again in 2019, and then lose my precious Nelia in November 2021.

Through it all, I have been surrounded by amazing family and friends, and a God that has been with me through it all!

So here we are. Everyone has a story, even me!

Iwo Jima

It was the Christmas season, and Walmart was crazy! People were coming and going! Every aisle was filled. I was taking an electric cart from the grocery entrance to the other door when I saw him. He was leaning against the wall and holding his walker. At first, I thought he was hurt, but then I realized he was just resting and waiting. His cap had just the word "veteran" on the bill, and I knew instantly he had to be World War II!

There aren't many World War II veterans left. The war ended nearly eighty years ago, and their numbers shrink every year. The United States had 416,800 casualties. Another 418,500 American civilians died. Worldwide casualties exceeded 15,000,000. There were 25,000,000 battle wounded. Global civilian deaths totaled 45,000,000. It was an awful war. It changed the lives forever of those that served. It lasted six years and one day. I was born two years before it ended, and I remember stories of the war. One of our neighbors had a son on the USS *Arizona* that was blown up in Pearl Harbor. He perished that day. My future brother-in-law quit high school with two of his classmates and joined the Navy. They lied about their ages, and were serving in the Pacific by their sixteenth birthdays. That was common. Many young men did that. Patriotism was everywhere! My brother-in-law never talked about the war. Whatever he saw…whatever he did…was buried inside him. That was so typical.

My father never served because of his injuries in the Oregon woods during the Depression, but we sacrificed as a family to support the war effort. That was also common. Everyone did their part any way they could. Food and tires and supplies were all rationed to support the troops. We raised most of the food we ate. It was a defining moment in history…a permanent molding of character. It is not an accident that it was called our "greatest generation".

Americans fought on foreign soil to protect people in countries that did not always speak our language, and didn't always embrace our values. They bled and died. They did it to save those people and their countries, and to prevent the war from coming to America. They were heroes!

As I approached him, I stopped my cart, and he looked at me. I saw the sacrifice etched in his face. I got off the cart and walked over to him, and asked him if he was a veteran. He said "yes", and I asked him when he served. He lowered his eyes as if he was mentally revisiting that time. Then he quietly said "World War II". I took his hand in mine, and said, "Thank you for your service". As we shook hands, he straightened up to his full height which was a couple inches taller than my 6 ft 1 inches. It was like something was happening inside his head…something special…remembering…As I held his hand, I thanked him again! It was a special moment for me too…a proud moment…a moment of remembering the cost of that war in blood and lives…just special! I was trying really hard not to tear up. I asked him how old he was. He said "93". By now, he was no longer holding on to the walker. He was someplace else. He was a soldier again. He would have been in his teens back then. I asked him where he served. The eyes dropped. It took a few moments for him to answer. Then he whispered, "Iwo Jima"! I said, "you are a hero!" He said, "No, the ones who didn't come home were the heroes." His eyes were moist.

There were MANY big battles in World War II. They were all bad. Iwo Jima was one of the biggest and bloodiest! It lasted from February 19, through March 26, 1945. The Allied forces needed a base near the Japanese coast. The island was guarded by 21,000-plus Japanese troops who were hidden in caves, tunnels, and all kinds of underground installations. Because they were so well-hidden, the American forces experienced little resistance when they first landed.

But when the Japanese attacked, the battle was furious and bloody. Much of the fighting was close and intense…sometimes hand to hand. The entire Island was only about nine square miles. Both sides were desperate! The US forces knew taking Iwo Jima was the key to defeating Japan and ending the war. The Japanese knew if they lost, Japan was going to be destroyed.

There were 110,000 total US forces. 6,821 would give their lives. Another 19,217 would be wounded. Many of the casualties were horrendous. The Japanese would record between 17,000 and 18,000 killed. Another 3,000 went into hiding and were not found. The final outcome was never in question because of overwhelming American superiority in numbers and support, especially from the Navy and Air Forces, but the victory would take five weeks. Twenty-seven Medals of Honor were presented later to Marines and sailors who fought there. Fourteen were presented posthumously. There were many heroes. All of us remember the graphic image of the six Marines raising the American flag in the picture taken by Joe Rosenthal. Three of those soldiers would die in action in the next few days while securing the island.

I turned away for a moment and looked around me. Dozens of customers were coming and going. Shopping was robust and intense. Suddenly, I JUST KNEW THIS MOMENT HAD TO BE SHARED!!! I called out to the shoppers closest to us. "Please take a moment and thank one of our nation's heroes! This man fought in the battle of Iwo Jima in World War II!" People just stopped! Then, a lady rushed up and hugged him and shook his hand. Others crowded around him, thanking him. One man saluted. All of a sudden people close by started clapping. In the midst of it all, his daughter returned from her shopping to witness it all. At first, she thought something had happened to him. When she realized what was taking place, she began crying. People were hugging her and thanking her for her father's sacrifice. Then it was over. People began moving on. The 93-year-old veteran and his daughter left the store, but his gait was a little faster…his back was a little straighter, and the season was a little brighter.

That was a special day in Walmart! That was a special day in the lives of a 93-year-old veteran and his proud daughter! It was a special day for the shoppers that got to witness it all! It was a special day in the life of a humble Walmart greeter who is STILL feeling grateful for all the blood that has been shed for our freedom!

The Day Sam Came to Town

Sam Walton always had a keen interest in Southeast Missouri. The low-key farm-oriented lifestyle was a perfect customer base for his retail store philosophy. His first store in Missouri was Sikeston, number nine in the Walmart chain.

The year was 1990, and Kevin was an associate at Caruthersville, just forty-five miles south of Sikeston. He had started his Walmart career four years earlier and had already been promoted to support manager. It was mid-morning when the call came in from the local airport that Sam Walton had just landed and needed a ride.

Kevin remembers that the store manager thought the call was a joke and didn't respond. About twenty minutes later, a second call came with a little more urgency. This time, the manager decided he'd better respond.

Sam Walton had a reputation for popping up at stores with no warning, and he had purchased a small single engine airplane which he flew himself. This was one of those trips. Kevin was dispatched to follow his manager to pick up Sam and his two passengers. Sam had brought two newly hired corporate buyers with him for the trip and to experience a Walmart retail store firsthand.

The manager loaded Sam into his car, and it was Kevin's job to transport the two buyers. Kevin drove a small 1990 Mazda regular cab pickup with floor mounted standard shift. The first buyer piled into the middle seat and volunteered to shift gears while Kevin operated the clutch pedal! According to Kevin, the second buyer looked like he was sick!

As soon as they were all loaded into the small truck, the second buyer immediately asked about renting a car in Caruthersville. Kevin explained that Caruthersville was just a small town, and there were no rental car agencies closer than St. Louis, a three-hour drive, or Memphis, Tennessee, located 90 minutes away. The buyer seemed desperate to get a car somehow. He even asked Kevin if he could drive them to their next destination which was Memphis, Tennessee. He said he did not want to fly another mile with Sam Walton as pilot!

On their trip from Bentonville, Arkansas to Kennett, Missouri, and on to Caruthersville, he told how Sam just loaded them into his plane and took off. He did NOT file a flight plan and just followed the highways to get to their destination in Kennett. The man was bordering on hysteria as he talked and said Sam would be flying and, if he decided to check out some store along the way, would turn the small plane from its flight path until he located the store from the air and then would circle while he counted cars in the parking lot. When he was satisfied, he would return to the highway and continue flying to the next stop. When he made these detours, he would whip out paperwork to check store data or whatever, and temporarily let the little plane fly itself! As the buyer told his story, his voice got louder and louder. Apparently, the straw that broke the camel's back came when they arrived in Kennett.

The Kennett airport is on the edge of town right behind a Dairy Queen. At the time, there was a power line that crossed the path at the beginning of the runway. Power lines like these always have large red balls on them so pilots will see them. As Sam had lined up with the runway to land the airplane and began his descent, the power line loomed larger and larger. Suddenly, he dipped the plane's nose and flew UNDER the powerline, then taxied the plane down the runway! This is a direct violation of FAA guidelines for pilots. As the poor buyer shared this last detail, he was nearly incoherent! The other buyer was content to just keep shifting gears while Kevin clutched! When they arrived at the Caruthersville store, the second buyer emphatically stated that he was not flying another mile with Sam Walton!

Sam Walton was already working his magic and charm as they entered the store. He got on the public address system and thanked customers and associates! He hugged store employees! He shook hands with customers! He autographed one-dollar bills! It was an event!

After spending an hour or two inspecting the store and visiting with associates and customers, they were off to their final destination of the day, Memphis. As Kevin drove the two buyers out to the tiny airport, the frightened buyer had apparently gotten a dose of courage, because he climbed back into the plane with Sam and the other buyer, and they flew off into the clear and beautiful blue Missouri sky—again with NO flight plan—to land in one of the larger international airports in the country!

It would be later reported that Sam just flew straight to Memphis and flew around until he spotted the huge airport. He then pointed the small plane at the runway and proceeded to land without even calling the control tower! After safely landing while dozens of other flights were hastily redirected, his license was reportedly promptly suspended. Kevin did not know whether the buyer lived through the landing!

By the time this story took place, Walmart had already grown into a worldwide retail phenomenon! From its founding in 1962, the company had grown to be the largest retailer in the United States. It was opening stores in Mexico, the U.K., Germany, China, Canada, and other countries, and was already the largest private employer in the world! Sales in 1990 totaled $26 billion.

As Kevin shared this story with me, as funny as it was, I could tell how meeting Sam Walton in person had impacted this young man so early in his career. Sam Walton had already accomplished more in business than anyone in our history. He was a billionaire sitting atop a worldwide empire when he flew into that tiny Missouri town in that small single engine airplane on that day in 1990. He spent time with the people he loved most—his customers and beloved associates.

Those Electric Carts!

Walmart furnishes electric carts for people with handicaps or disabilities. However, there are a lot of people using these carts that are not disabled, but we are not allowed to say anything. Sometimes, it is entertaining. I sometimes watch people walk across the parking lot with no problem, then everything changes when they get to the automatic doors.

They get these pained looks on their faces. They will develop limps or have trouble walking. Their breathing will become heavy. They will stoop over. They will look to the cart, and then back to me. Then, they will look back at the cart as if it is calling out their name. They will hobble to the cart, and struggle to get on it. As they drive away, they seem to get better until they return. It makes me want to ask Walmart to station a doctor near the front doors.

These carts cost a lot of money. They have signs all over them that tell customers not to take them outside, but these people who manage to walk into the store can't make it back to their cars. I have no issues with the truly handicapped, but I watch customers take carts outside every day, leave them all over the place, then get off them and walk to their cars with no difficulty. If they leave them inside, they will go away without plugging them in. Then, the next customer gets a cart that has not been charged if we don't notice it. Practically all truly handicapped people take time to plug their carts in if they are able. They will usually try to alert me if they are not able.

My first wife had severe congestive heart failure, and my second wife suffered a severe stroke, so I have real empathy for the people that depend on these carts. But I get so frustrated at the people that are just too lazy to walk as they shop and just jump on a cart.

The people that are the worst are those that think an electric cart is their birthright! They will say cheerful things like "Get me a cart!" "Why aren't there any carts?" "That lady isn't handicapped…see if she will give me her cart!" "Go to the other end and see if there's a cart!" "I need one NOW!" That said, I have NEVER been treated rudely by a person who was truly handicapped.

I have shared electric cart stories in other chapters in this book. One story I haven't shared is about an extremely obese man that always parked in the first handicapped parking space closest to the grocery door. He would park and sit in his car until someone rode their cart outside, and he would get them to park right next to his driver door. He would hobble the one or two step to the cart while putting most of his weight on the car door, then drop himself onto the cart.

Then, he would ride the cart into the store and do his shopping. He always filled his cart to overflowing. He would always check out in the grocery self-check, and when he was ready to exit the store, he would always get an associate to go out to his car with him to load his purchases into his car. Then, after he got into his car, they would bring the electric cart back inside for him.

One day, after he had exited the self-check area and was headed to his car, a sharp-eyed cashier came over to me and told me she didn't think he had scanned all his purchases. Everything was always bagged, so we were never able to receipt check him.

I reported the incident to asset protection. They reviewed video of the purchase and reported that he had, in fact, only scanned a handful of the items in his cart, and they were all inexpensive items. He pretended to drag all the other items across the scanner and put every item in a bag. He obviously knew that we were not allowed to inspect bagged merchandise.

Improvements have been made and this couldn't happen now since they have replaced all the checkout registers. Cashiers also now have a small hand held computer scanner device and they can watch all the purchases being scanned at every self-check register in their area.

We were on alert the next time he came into the store. Watching him was not difficult, because he always took several hours to complete his shopping.

On this particular day, when he was through, he rode his cart around the self-check area and rode into the room where we sold our liquor at the time. Liquor was moved to the rear of the grocery area after the store was remodeled.

He must have been watching me somehow, because when I pretended to get busy away from the door area, he tried to ride his cart toward the door. I intercepted him and reminded him that carts were not allowed beyond the registers until purchases had been checked out and paid for.

He circled around the self-check and found a register. The same cashier that had alerted me before was on duty, and she was watching everything he did. Asset protection was also monitoring everything.

He scanned every single item in the cart, and then spent about thirty minutes trying to pay for everything. Finally, he called the cashier over and canceled everything except for one item that cost less than $2.00.

All of the merchandise left behind was taken to the service desk and tabulated. The total was over $400.00. We never saw him in the store again after that day. I am pretty sure he had been stealing from us regularly for over two years!

All that time, I had never receipt checked him because I felt sorry for him! He taught me a valuable lesson! Thieves can ride an electric cart. Since then, I have caught several other people on carts that were trying to steal.

There are so many stories I have witnessed on those carts. I remember another day when we were having issues with the inner grocery door exit. We had turned the automatic door off, so that it wouldn't open and shut. I had set up two hazard cones on each side of the closed door, so people would not enter or exit.

A young couple came into the store, and the girl had one leg in a walking cast. She was using one crutch, and she had her cell phone clutched in her other free hand and glued to her ear. She climbed onto one of our electric carts and drove off into the store. The phone never left her ear.

Thirty or forty minutes later, I saw her headed into the grocery self-check, phone stuck to her ear, talking nonstop. It took longer than normal for her to check out, because she remained seated on the cart the entire time and continued to chatter away through the entire time.

Finally, I saw her finishing up, and preparing to leave the store. As she exited the self-check area, still talking nonstop, I got distracted by a customer needing directions for an item in the store. As I was looking it up on my Walmart app, I heard this loud crash behind me! When I say it was a LOUD crash, I mean it was a REALLY LOUD CRASH! Everything momentarily stopped at the grocery end of Walmart!

We all turned around, and there was this young woman, sitting on the cart, half-in and half-out the door, knocked open by the cart. Cones on both sides of the now partially open door were knocked over in total disarray, and she sat in the middle of all of this, looking dazed, and still on her phone!

As I ran up, she was trying to explain to whoever she was talking to, what she thought had happened. Her husband came running up, got her purchases out of the cart, and helped her up. She grabbed her crutch with her one free hand and continued her conversation!

I watched her and her husband as they left the store and walked across the parking lot. He looked like he had been through this before! I wondered who was on the call with her. It had to be someone important, maybe the president! Whoever it was, she was still talking on the phone!

I put the cones back and closed the door, shaking my head. It's Walmart!

I'm always having to chase kids off the carts. I remember an incident when I watched two young girls race each other across the parking lot. As they made their entrance, one of the girls started to limp badly and walk straight to an electric cart. When I stopped her, she told me she had hurt her leg at school.

I reminded her that it had not kept her from running across the parking lot. She burst out laughing, and said, "Oh, you saw me?" The limp was instantly healed, and she and her friend went on into Walmart, looking back, occasionally, and laughing. I just waved and smiled.

Another time, a customer came in, and told me she had just come from the store a block away across the street. She said four young boys were playing on our carts in the other store's parking lot. Someone at the other entrance had not been paying attention, and they had managed to get all four carts outside Walmart, across our parking lot, across the street, and into the other store's parking lot.

I got permission to retrieve the carts and went after them. When I hollered at the boys, they jumped off and took off running. Party over!

Not all kids are as easy to handle. When they come in small gangs, they can be difficult to manage. That's when management or the police are called.

The many nice people that depend and use these carts make up for all the rude people. I have made many friends. I make it a practice to meet some of them who are having real difficulty getting across the parking lot and into the store. When I see them, if I am not busy, I will hop on a cart and bring it to them. That appreciative smile makes up for all those things we put up with at the front door!

The store has had from eight to fourteen electric carts in service at different times. If we had one hundred, it would not be enough because of all the abuse by people that don't really need them. I am grateful we have these carts. There are many aging or disabled shoppers that would not be able to take care of their weekly needs without this Walmart courtesy. They are not without their problems, but we do our best! It's Walmart!

Thou Shalt Not Steal

I learned those words before I started grade school! My parents drilled me on that principle all through my formative years. When you are hired at Walmart, theft is covered over and over. The company has a zero tolerance for ANY kind of theft. We are coached to be on the alert for customer theft, but also theft by associates. If an employee is caught stealing ANY amount, they are subject to immediate termination with no chance of ever working for Walmart again. Sadly, there are still associates and customers who do steal.

One of the unpleasant parts of my job is to catch thieves by checking receipts. On one occasion, an associate who had yet to reach his twenty-first birthday chose to sacrifice his job and future for $4.67! He apparently felt that Walmart owed him his lunch. He had left his workstation in self-check to take his lunch break, gone to the deli and ordered a sandwich, and then went directly to the Subway located at our entrance to finish his lunch break. I walked into the Subway and asked to see his receipt for the sandwich. He lied and told me he had thrown it away. About thirty minutes later, he came up to me and told me he had found it. When I looked at the receipt which was date and time stamped, I noticed that the time was just three minutes earlier! He had purchased a SECOND sandwich to cover his lie! I was already struggling over saying something to management, but that second lie told me I had no choice! It was the first time I turned in an associate. I still feel physically sick! It is not easy to turn in someone you have worked with every day. But zero tolerance is zero tolerance. If theft is ignored, people do it again, and others see it, and they steal. A few days later, I heard he had been terminated. Why does this happen?

I remember receipt checking a retired lady riding one of our electric carts. She had her grandson with her who was about five or six years old. I was watching her check out at one of our self-check registers and saw her scan a package of pencils three times, but each time she bagged a pair of children's shoes! When I confronted her, she accused the little boy of losing her receipts. As we walked down to customer service, the little fellow was in tears. The theft totaled $73.00. We took the high road and gave her the chance of paying for the merchandise or returning it. She ended up paying for one pair of shoes and a toy that she had failed to scan earlier, then returned the rest. I am sure she had stolen before, and I am sure she will steal again. Her theft was deliberate and scheming. Why does this happen?

Every day, someone tries to steal something somewhere in the store. No department is safe, but cosmetics and pharmaceuticals are particularly vulnerable, with many small items easy to conceal in purses and clothing. Why is this happening???

I checked two teenage girls one Friday night, and one of them had a candy bar in the bag along with one other item. I had watched her pick-up the candy bar as she walked into self-check. Her purchase cost about $3.00. She paid with a $10 dollar bill…more than enough to pay for the candy bar, but she chose to steal it instead. When I stopped her, she just went back and paid for it. She claimed she "forgot" even though she had picked it up less than thirty seconds before she began her check out. Why???

One of my favorite stories took place during a Christmas season. I saw a man drop off two ladies who came in and sat waiting on a bench inside our entrance. A few minutes later, he came in and asked me if I had noticed a cart outside the door with a new television loaded in it. He was a "good Samaritan" neighbor who had brought the elderly mother (she was 92) and her daughter to Walmart to return the tv they had bought earlier that day for a different one. Someone had taken the cart and television while he was parking his car. I took him to security where they reviewed camera footage. The video showed the thieves taking the cart and loading the tv into their parked car. When Walmart "zoomed" in on the car, they were able to read the license number. Police intercepted the car when it pulled into the thief's driveway, arrested him, and recovered the television! In the meantime, Walmart was doing its part. When management heard about the incident, they stepped in and GAVE a second television to this lady! Only a handful of people knew of this act of kindness. I felt really good about my job that night and the company that signed my paycheck!

I could go on and on. Practically every one of our cashiers has at least one story. People steal from Walmart every day. They are old and young. They are thin and fat. They are white and black and yellow and red. They are males and females. They work alone or in groups or pairs. They are poor and rich! Some are customers, and some are associates. People steal from Walmart every day! Why?

If they steal from Walmart, they are stealing in other places as well! It may be merchandise…it may be minutes on a time clock at work… it may be a pencil or copy paper at work…and on and on…why?

I had a college minor in psychology, so "why" has always fascinated me. There are lots of "whys" involving stealing.

Kleptomania is a compulsion for stealing…getting a rush…the thrill! It is rarely for personal gain. If identified, it can be treated. Years ago, when I owned my dealership in St. Louis, I had a manager whose wife was a kleptomaniac. He was my used car manager, and he just left the dealership several times without any explanation. He was directly responsible for eight used car salesmen and all used car appraisals for both the new and used car departments. His absence left a huge hole in operations. His unexcused absence was a violation of company policy and subject to discipline or dismissal. When I called him in to discuss his behavior, he broke down and started crying. He told me that he had been going to pick up his wife after she was arrested for shoplifting. This was happening several times a month. She also worked, and their combined income was over

$120,000, and she was shoplifting! They had EVERYTHING…a beautiful home…two wonderful sons…LOTS of stuff…nice furniture…expensive cars…a boat…THE AMERICAN DREAM…and she was a thief!!! I gave him some paid time off to arrange for some professional help for his wife, and with therapy and treatment, she got her life together which saved their marriage and family. That experience left an indelible impression on me…heartbreaking…but I give thanks to God that this life was saved!

Addiction-related stealing is the result of a dependency on drugs or gambling, etc. It is rarely meant to harm anyone, but rather fills a need. It may be emotional. It may be literal. When the addiction is admitted and treated, the stealing usually stops. Over the years, I have had several employees who were addicts. I have worked beside people who are addicts. The biggest problem, in addition to their addiction, is practically ALWAYS self-denial! They are convinced they can control their addiction without help and practically always have to hit bottom before they get help. I once had a used car salesman that was my top producer, but once or twice a year, he would take some time off and fly to Las Vegas. He was a compulsive gambler. He would stay until he had lost everything…ALL his money! One day when he came back, he told me about being up in his winnings over $150,000 before he lost it all. Sometimes, it would take a couple days. One time, it took just a couple hours. He was compulsive…and sick. With the help of his girlfriend (he had destroyed his first marriage), we convinced him to get professional help. He ended up getting his life together and eventually was promoted to management. I give thanks to God that this life was saved!

There is pathological stealing. This type of stealing is not meant to intentionally harm anyone. It just fills a need, emotionally or literally, and it can also be treated.

There is non-pathological stealing which is, sometimes, just taking care of basic needs…no food at home…homeless…desperation stealing. Sometimes, non-pathological stealing takes a "peer pressure" turn…hanging out with the wrong crowd…the thrill of pulling it off.

Sometimes it is a "I didn't think it through, or I wouldn't have done it". This type of stealing fills an emotional need. "I steal because I can!" It's exciting! It's challenging! It satisfies a greed, and then it doesn't!

Books have been written about stealing. Studies have been done on stealing. The common denominator in ALL these reasons for stealing…for taking something that belongs to someone else…is that they are ALL wrong! Since the beginning of civilization, it has been considered wrong to take something from others without their permission. It is one of the Ten Commandments! "You shall not steal" (Exodus 20, v. 8). It is WRONG!

I remember a time as a little boy. It was a Saturday. Every Saturday, Mom loaded us in the car along with the eggs that had been gathered that week and the cream that had been separated, and we headed to town. After dropping off the cream and eggs, we would head to my aunt's home, and Mom would give each of us a nickel that we could spend on ANYTHING! We headed for Daugherty's drug store and had soon spent our money. As we were leaving the store, we noticed some "penny" candy near the door. It was just too enticing! We looked around, and nobody was paying us any attention, so we helped ourselves to some candy and walked out. When we returned to my aunt's, we were enjoying our candy. Mom came over and asked to see our treasures. We proudly showed her our purchases. Then, I had one of those experiences that shape lives and values! My mother quietly began adding up our purchases and asked how we were able to afford the candy. There wasn't enough money! We were exposed! She didn't yell. She didn't spank us. She just talked to us about stealing. She just talked to us about the ten commandments. And then she did the unthinkable! She told us we had to go back to the drugstore and apologize to Mr. Daugherty for what we had done! We had to go alone! I have some appreciation for convicts walking to their execution! That was the longest two blocks in my young life. I remember going inside and timidly asking to speak to Mr. Daugherty. I was praying he wouldn't call the sheriff! But to Mr. Daugherty's eternal credit, he simply shook our hands, and thanked us for doing the "right" thing and told us to not steal again. I never did!

It's when I see stealing now in Walmart that I notice, more than ever, the breakdown of the family unit in today's society…too many single-family households…a lack of moral guideposts…no mother that will quietly recite the ten commandments to her children… cutting corners. It makes me sad, and it reminds me that it all starts with me! We never know when our example will change another's life! Each one of us must shoulder the burden! Each one of us must be the example! You shall not steal! Thanks, Mom! Thanks, Mr. Daugherty!

It's appropriate that I finish this chapter on a high note! Everyday as I stand at the front door, someone comes up the front door looking embarrassed and asks to go back in the store to pay for something they missed.

The other day, I had a first! A young woman walked up to me with her young son. He looked about five or six years old. She was obviously upset and acting almost angry. She demanded to speak to the manager. I offered to take her inside, and she got very agitated, and said the manager needed to meet her OUTSIDE the store!

By then, I knew this was not a normal complaint, so I asked her what we needed to do to help her. She angrily told me she and her son had just left the store. While she had been shopping, he had slipped off by himself and stolen a package of gum.

His theft was exposed when they got home, and she informed me that they were not coming back into Walmart until he had returned his stolen merchandise and apologized!

Management was quickly summoned, apologies were given, stolen merchandise was returned, and stern lectures were delivered while mother insisted that the tearful offender look the manager in the eye!

Finally, a handshake was exchanged along with a promise never to steal again, tears were dried, and mom and son walked off to their car. She had her arm around him.

Thank God for moms that care! Thank God for the millions of responsible people in the world who don't steal!

Those Amazing Associates!

In forty-plus years of hiring and managing employees, I have NEVER seen such diversity as is illustrated every day at Walmart. These incredible people literally come from everywhere. Every day, I see tattoos. I see orange and blue and red and green hair! I see woven braids. I see the very young (sixteen and up), the very old (employees in the 80s), and everything in between. I see black, white, red, and yellow. I see high school dropouts and those with college educations. I see EVERYTHING! Walmart takes this cross section of humanity who would probably have nothing in common outside the store, and molds them into a cohesive and dynamic workforce that has revolutionized retail. I feel like they are my extended family. Breaks in the lunchroom are fascinating to watch! People from every walk of life sit down in a common bond and share!

Raised by her grandparents, Latazia's story should inspire anyone! This young woman went on to college after graduating from high school. She is married and has four delightful children! The oldest was twelve and the youngest under eight when Latazia first started working for Walmart! I love it when they come to the store! Her Walmart story began just four short years ago in electronics as a part time associate. A smart manager promoted her to customer service manager in just five months! Latazia balances being a good wife/mother/dedicated associate career in amazing fashion! Walmart is a crazy place! There is ALWAYS something happening! People are everywhere! It's stressful! She is ALWAYS smiling! She is ALWAYS quietly leading! Her smile inspires MY smile! And she is leaving…but not leaving Walmart! She has been promoted to Assistant Manager and is being reassigned to a metro Kansas City Superstore next week…in just four years!!!! Walmart will be paying her moving expenses and the first month's rent! Kansas City is about to get better!!!! With hard work and dedication, she is on the road to co-manager and maybe her own store!!!

There's another associate that I LOVED to watch! She was like magic as she did her job! She had worked for Walmart long enough to have met Sam Walton several times. Her voice changed when she described those encounters. "Mr. Walton loved his customers!" "He loved associates!" "He really cared about us!" "He took my hand and looked right into my face and gave me a great big smile and thanked me"! She told how he flew his plane into the local airport and had the store manager pick him up for his store visits. Sam Walton died in 1992. It was special to witness the reverence shared by an associate so many years later.

"Ms. Magic" stood at her register five days a week! She was smiling! Her bubbling personality radiated as she scanned each customer's merchandise! I watched customers seek out her register. They KNEW they were going to get out of the store faster if she checked them out! She would make a comment now and then, and customers will smile, but mostly she just went like the energizer bunny…working her magic…making everyone around her feel like the most important people in the store. When she went home, she divided her time between her church and making a difference by helping others! She had a big heart and shared it! Walmart and the world were lucky to have her!

There is a sad ending to this associate's story. After thirty-eight years serving Walmart's customers, Ms. Magic was eased into retirement. From my vantage point, it looked more like she was pushed. Sometimes, big companies can seem sort of heartless. I know there are two sides to these kinds of stories, but I didn't like this one! The good news is that she is still serving her community through her church and sometimes on her own. As long as there is someone in need, she will pop up somewhere! This was Walmart's loss! I think Sam would agree with me! I ask people about her from time to time. She is still that special lady just doing God's work and taking care of others.

Chris and Teddy were stockmen. Stockmen are in a class by themselves! That means they work outside in all kinds of weather gathering shopping carts and bringing them inside. I have seen them in the rain and in blowing snow. It can be a tough job! They are always happy! Well, most of the time, they are happy. They are also responsible for trash on the lot. Chris just graduated from high school and Teddy was a senior. Walmart is great about working with part-time workers and their personal schedules. We have many college students who work part-time. Chris just transferred to another Walmart store in a town with a four-year college. He would continue working for Walmart there while he pursued a degree in marketing.

Teddy never met a girl he didn't like! They all liked him too!

I have gotten to meet lots of stockmen! This job probably has the highest turnover of any position at Walmart. Most of these guys come in like Superman. They practically jog after those carts! They will grunt and strain while they push fifteen or twenty carts into the cart bay. Then, they will flex their muscles (not allowed), or come into the store for a bottle of water and return an hour later (not allowed) There are a lot of places you can hide in a 235,000 square foot store. You can stop and talk or flirt with another associate in one of the dozens of shopping aisles (not allowed), or you can go into one of the restrooms. You can just screw around in the store killing time (not allowed). Sometimes, you can get creative.

One day, during Covid when they had me working outside, I watched four stockmen change a customer's tire in handicapped parking. The best part was watching them look for the jack. In my forty-plus years in the car business, I learned that automobile manufacturers can get pretty creative in hiding jacks!

They would take turns digging in the cargo area. After a few minutes, there would be a conference. One of the guys was doing NO physical labor, but he seemed to be in charge in the conferences. I'm pretty sure he's management material! They never did find the jack.

Finally, one of them went to his personal vehicle and returned with his own jack. While he was gone, two of the guys decided to smoke a cigarette (not allowed). The "manager" got on his cell phone (not allowed). When the guy with the jack returned, there was a flurry of activity. The manager got off his phone and got back to managing. Two of the guys went to work getting the doughnut spare out of the cargo compartment.

That was fun to watch! The guy with the jack went to work getting the car up in the air! He got the flat tire off the wheel, and then the party started! All four of these guys bent over and around that wheel lifting that little doughnut spare! Butt cracks were visible everywhere! I just knew someone was going to knock that car off the jack, but somehow, they managed to get the tire on the wheel, tighten the lug nuts, and let the jack back down.

By now, both cart bays had been empty for some time, and customers were going out on the lot getting their own carts. I heard quite a bit of uncensored advice from some as they charged back into the store. The four cart pushers spent a few minutes congratulating each other on doing a good deed, and then they slowly walked back out and began pushing carts again.

We never did get caught up with carts again that day, but hey … It's Walmart!!!

Walmart gets large truckloads of merchandise every day. These trucks have to be unloaded, and the merchandise needs to be put on stock shelves or out front in the store to be sold. The teams that handle this process work hard and fast! Walmart allows a fifteen minute break every two hours, and these teams tend to take their breaks in unison, coming and going together.

For some reason one day, as the afternoon team was heading outside to the designated smoking area for their fifteen-minute break, I hollered out, "The A team is leaving the building!" The reaction was immediate and electric! There was loud laughter and some high fives, and then something special happened! Everybody was walking a little straighter and with a little more pride! Everybody felt good!

So, when they came back in from their break, I shouted, "The A team is entering the building!" And just like that, they became the "A" team. It was not a surprise to see that the additional recognition and positive encouragement affected the whole attitude of this team! Since that day, when any of that team come through the front door, they get an "A team" cheer, and I get a little bit of a lift for making others feel better about themselves! I love the A team!

I remember Betty and Lula. They were both *senior*, senior citizens, still working because they had too. Betty was eighty and Lula was eighty-four. Walmart is really good about hiring senior citizens. If you can meet their physical and mental requirements, you have a good chance of getting hired.

Betty worked in apparel and always had something good to say to anyone. She was small but feisty. I remember the day her son came in and told me she had just been diagnosed with cancer. When I saw her later that day, she seemed to want to talk about it, so I listened. She talked about her family. She talked about the cancer and told me it was not good. We talked a little about Jesus and her faith. She broke down a couple times. I remember holding her hand and sharing a short prayer. I asked God to give her strength and comfort her. I asked Him to surround her with that Love and Peace which surpasses our human understanding. I remember our hug. She didn't work much more after that day. She would come into Walmart now and then with one of her kids, and we would always chat, but the cancer was eating away at her body, and she was so frail. She passed away a few days later.

Lula was a cashier. She worked for Walmart over twenty-five years, lived alone, and she didn't have any children. Her family was really her brother and sister, Walmart associates, and her church. She was tiny like Betty. She was quiet and polite. She did her job well and with pride. She never missed work. I would sometimes convince her to let me help her load her car when she bought bigger things. I remember our last conversation. We were talking about how long we would keep working. She told me Walmart was her life. She didn't know what she would do if she was not working. She said she would probably keep working until God told her it was time to quit. We left it at that.

A few weeks later, she was shopping at a small store across the street from Walmart, and just collapsed. She was transported to St. Louis after suffering a brain hemorrhage but never recovered.

I know Heaven broke out in song when these two ladies came Home! I brings me comfort when I think of these little ladies singing in Heaven's chorus. I thank God for letting me be a small part of their lives! They made Walmart a better place to work! They made our world a better place to live!

There are so many more that have come and gone. There are so many more that have become good friends. There's Ginger and Vicki, and Roxanne and Andrea. There's Teresa and John and Tina and Penny. There's Kathy and Marilyn and Kim. There's Carolyn and Becky and Greg and Stephen. There are so many more! Maybe I will write another book someday just about Walmart associates!

The more I talk to these amazing people, the more I am reminded how much EACH ONE of them matters. I wish I could interview every one of them! They ALL have stories! These amazing people come from everywhere. They have different talents and beliefs. Many of them would not have met outside our walls, and Walmart takes them and molds them into this cohesive work force that has changed the world of retail.

They have children who attend our schools. They fill our churches. They volunteer. They serve their communities. They spend money all over their towns where they live. They pay taxes which build roads and bridges and support our government. They matter…to Walmart…to their communities…to our country…to the world!

Economists say that a company's payroll will turn about six or seven times each year in the local economy. Walmart would not share payroll information with me, but I estimated my store's payroll at approximately thirteen million dollars annually. That means that it has an annual impact of about ninety million every year to the surrounding area. Worldwide, Walmart employs more than 2.3 million associates. Seventy-five percent of Walmart's management started as hourly associates. Every manager in my store, except one, started as an hourly employee. Corporate annual sales were close to $642 billion in the last fiscal year. As a manager and business owner, I learned early that a company's most valuable asset is its employee base. They do not show up anywhere on a financial statement or balance sheet, but they are critical to a company's success! No company can survive without good people. I am surrounded by them every day! I LOVE MY JOB!!!

Birthdays

Birthdays are a big deal! Birthdays are a really big deal if you are a kid! Mothers get all funny and giddy when one of their kids is celebrating a birthday!

I get to see this up close and in person every day at Walmart when I am checking receipts at the door. Birthdays are usually pretty easy to spot. The big tip-off is the box from bakery. Cake boxes are different from all the other bakery boxes.

Sometimes, it will be something else...cupcakes, party paper plates or napkins, a special toy or two. There is always a tip-off!

One day, a young mother approached me with her three little kids, and I saw this birthday cake in the shopping cart. As I took her receipt and began checking it, I pointed at the cake, and asked, "What's this?" "That's this one's birthday cake. Today is her birthday!" and she pointed at one of her children.

Something came over me! That little girl was smiling SO big as her mother was pointing at HER! You could tell she was excited about her birthday, and her brother and sister were excited as well. Mom was beaming at all three!

This moment needed to be shared! I leaned over that little girl as her mother looked on, and asked her, "Is it REALLY your birthday?"

She looked up at me in the most beautiful innocent angelic way, and shyly said, "Yes"! The smile melted my heart! I knew this moment had to be shared!

Four years of college applied voice training, performing hundreds of vocal solos and singing in vocal ensembles has honed my voice. It's hard to explain, but it penetrates! It is the largest voice in the room. Over the years, when I have needed to bring a crowd to silence, all I had to do was raise my voice. When my first wife was still alive, and I would whisper something to her, she would always say, "Why are you whispering? The whole world can hear you anyway!"

This was one of those moments! The whole world needed to celebrate this sweet little girl's birthday, at least the Sikeston, Missouri Walmart world! In a very soft voice, I asked her if it was okay to share her birthday with all our friends at Walmart. She shyly smiled and nodded her head. I looked at her mother, and mom nodded too.

I told mom to get out her cell phone. The world was about to celebrate her daughter's birthday.

I wrapped my arm around the little girl's tiny shoulders, and we moved over to where we were visible to all the people checking out at the registers. We were standing where grocery shoppers could see us as well.

In my big voice, I shouted, "Ladies and gentlemen, we have a birthday to celebrate! Sarah is eight years old TODAY!!! We are going to sing Happy Birthday to her TOGETHER!"

For just a few seconds, everything paused at Walmart that morning! People stopped their shopping carts and looked toward that loud voice. Cashiers and customers all turned and saw us standing there. Then, as I began to sing, people all around us were smiling and singing too! In just a few seconds, a busy store had been transformed into a happy joyous celebration of a little girl's birthday! Mother recorded it all on her phone! The smile on that little girl's face would light a room. The sounds of singing could be heard throughout the front half of the store. As we were singing, an elderly lady walked over and handed the little girl a five-dollar bill as she whispered, "Happy birthday." I saw the mother tearing up. A better birthday moment could not have been orchestrated.

As mother and her kids exited the store, I could hear them laughing and talking! The little girl still squeezed that bill tightly in her hand. A whole lot of happiness was everywhere! An older man approached me as he left the self-check area. He was smiling and he told me, "That little girl is going to remember this moment the rest of her life!" Several people told me it was the best thing they had ever seen at Walmart!

It felt really good helping to create a very special moment for a little girl and her family and a store full of busy stressed shoppers who would spend the rest of their day smiling about an unforgettable moment at Walmart!

That crazy fun moment has been recreated many times since that day. Everyone is different, but they always end the same. The instant joy that comes from those occasions always fills the store with smiles and happiness. Customers are enjoying their shopping experience just a little more, and another birthday leaves the store with an unforgettable life memory!

A few months after that first spontaneous birthday celebration, one of our coaches surprised me and took my picture which she posted on the Walmart website on Facebook with a short post about our birthday celebrations. I checked it out again later. It had been liked or loved 595 times, drawn 156 comments, and had been shared 90 times!!! People love it when we celebrate birthdays!!!

Birthday celebrations have caught on with our associates too. Now, when an associate is celebrating a birthday, another associate usually tracks me down, and we spread a little bit of joy among ourselves with the help of a whole lot of shopping strangers!

When I came to work at Walmart several years ago, I made myself a promise that every person who came through those doors was going to receive a smile. Smiles matter! The world needs more smiles! Smiles make our world a better place!

Helping someone celebrate their birthday has provided me with another venue for accomplishing my goal. The smiles are everywhere!!! Getting a bunch of strangers to join together in song while giving another stranger an unforgettable memory puts a smile on my heart!

Obesity

America is fat! Nowhere is that more apparent than Walmart. Our electric carts have a weight limit of 350 pounds, including purchases. That weight limit is exceeded over fifty percent of the time.

I had heart bypass surgery twenty-one years ago. In 2008, I had to have two stents put in my heart. In 2018, I was diagnosed as borderline diabetic. I remember the conversation with my doctor. I asked him what caused type 2 diabetes. He asked me my age, weight, and height. I remember telling him I was six feet, one inch tall and weighed 257 pounds.

He is a personal friend and a member of my church. He consulted a chart and informed me I was obese for my age! Anything over 227 pounds was considered obese.

That made me mad! No one had EVER called me obese before. He was not trying to be rude or insulting to me. He was just doing his job as a physician and telling his patient the truth.

I set a goal for myself that very day to get my weight down to 200 pounds, and soon! He got me an appointment with an on-staff dietitian, and she gave me thirty-seven pages of boring dietary information, but three pages changed my life. They talked about portions. They talked about carbohydrates. They talked about healthy snacks.

I immediately started watching the amount of food I was eating every day. I ate the same foods as before, but I simply ate less. I kept my carbohydrate intake under fifty grams. And, finally, I began eating a healthy snack in the mid-morning and mid-afternoon. Those three things produced dramatic results.

In less than six months, I lost fifty-eight pounds. I was now a healthy 199 pounds and feeling better than I had felt in years. Unfortunately, it did not contain the diabetes, but it has made it easier to treat. So far, I have been able to keep it under control by watching my diet and maintaining my weight. Six years later, my weight stays between 200 and 210 pounds.

It has become a joke in the break room guessing how many grapes I will eat in my snack! I don't care! Those snacks have created many opportunities to encourage others to watch their diet.

I drink practically no alcohol, get plenty of rest, try to watch my stress levels, conduct a simple exercise routine four to five times a week, and walk between twenty and thirty miles every week. Most people think I am ten to twenty years younger than my eighty-one years.

According to Wikipedia, a 2019 survey concluded that about forty percent of the American population is obese, and eighteen percent are severely obese. About half of our population has some type of heart disease, and a little over nine percent are diabetic. One in three Americans are considered pre-diabetic. These statistics have the potential of bankrupting our healthcare system if they are not addressed. Health.com reports that more than fourteen percent of Americans suffering from diabetes spend over forty percent of their income after food and housing on insulin.

I am pretty sure most of those people show up at Walmart every day. When they leave the store, their carts are filled with junk food and soda. Recently, a lady that easily weighed over 300 pounds approached me on an electric cart. The cart was filled with heavily breaded frozen entrees, junk food, and 12 six packs of Pepsi Cola. I asked her if she was planning a party. She laughed and said she didn't have any vices. She just liked soda! She laughed again when she told me she would see me next week! When I checked her receipt, most of the groceries were paid with food stamps. Taxpayer dollars are helping this woman to an early grave! Statistically, she will live ten years shorter because of her lifestyle.

A few months ago, an associate came up to me and asked if he could take an electric cart to a customer who was stranded in the grocery section on another electric cart. Our carts rarely stop working unless they have used up their charge, so I climbed on another electric cart and followed him to the customer.

As soon as I saw the stranded shopper, I was positive I knew the problem. The man sitting on the cart had to be well over 400 pounds. The cart was holding two cases of soda and five gallons of bottled water. His wife was standing beside him, holding on to a regular shopping cart piled high with nothing but junk food, more soda, and a bunch of prepared frozen entrees. I looked at the cart and saw practically nothing that could be considered healthy. She was probably over three hundred pounds herself.

I looked at the man, and he was just sitting there. I suggested moving the sodas to the woman's cart, and he just nodded. We transferred them, but the cart still didn't budge.

There is no polite way to tell a man he is too fat, so I asked the man if he was able to stand and let me try to operate the cart. He got up slowly and stepped aside.

I climbed on the cart, still loaded with the water. It took right off, operating normally. I turned to the man, and told him, "Sir, I'm sorry. You and your groceries may have exceeded the weight limit on this cart."

Both he and his wife had already figured that out. He just gave me a resigned look without speaking, and shuffled off with his wife, leaving the water behind. The associate and I returned the two electric carts to the front of the store.

This gentleman was an extreme example, but every day we have extremely obese customers come in and ride these carts. Many are under sixty-five and on disability. Most are covered by Medicare or Medicaid. When we check their receipts, an alarming number are receiving some social benefits. Our government is subsidizing obesity!

When I go to the break room, I am dismayed by the number of associates that are eating junk food and drinking sodas on their breaks.

It is a national crisis! There is no way to sugar coat this chapter (no pun intended). We MUST find a way to solve this disgraceful and preventable situation. We are rapidly approaching the zero hour!

Those Sagging Pants!

If you go to Walmart, sagging pants are everywhere! I stand at the front door and watch these young men come in. Sometimes, I see an older man trying to be young again with his pants sagging. It doesn't work very well!

They sort of waddle. If they walk normally, their pants fall down. What results is a sort of sub primal duck walk without the quacking. They purposefully buy them too large, and then they don't wear belts.

I have become an authority on all the varieties of undershorts and patterns. Some like solid colors. It really doesn't matter, the end result is always the same! Lots of rear end hanging out!

Every generation has its fads. I remember the duck tail haircuts, and the sideburns down to the navel...white socks...sunglasses, but showing off your undershorts? I've heard the stories about prison, and lowering your pants, but showing your rear end in Walmart? Disgusting!!!

The really amazing thing is how people pretend to ignore it, even though I have found hardly anyone who likes it. Walmart has a posted policy that men must wear shirts and shoes, but they allow men and boys to walk around or ride carts with their butts hanging out! Disgusting!

I am pretty sure that a posted policy that underwear cannot be visible would cure the embarrassing sight in a minute with barely a ripple in sales. I don't expect any change in policy any time soon.

We are not allowed to say anything, but every now and then, I slip. I could lose my job. I remember three such incidents.

The first one happened several years ago. It was late one night, and we weren't very busy. I looked up at the grocery entrance and saw these three young men entering the store. To say that their pants were hanging low is being kind. Their pants were so low that I could see their undershorts from the front! Gravity was barely being denied!

Adrenalin immediately overpowered common sense, and as they approached me, I angrily told them, "Pull up your pants!"

I got three angry and insolent stares, and they pulled their pants up...sort of. I could no longer see their undershorts from the front!

The little man inside my head was screaming! "NO!!! You are not allowed to do that!" The adrenaline was quickly settling down and being replaced with a healthy dose of remorse and gratitude that no manager had been lurking close by. I said a silent prayer that nobody would be too interested in replaying videos from those cameras always smiling down on me.

About twenty minutes later, I saw them leaving the customer service area and preparing to leave the store. They were headed directly toward me.

When they got about ten feet from me, the one in the middle dropped his pants all the way to his ankles. All three of them burst into wild laughter.

The adrenaline took over again, and I looked straight at the young man and quietly said, "It's a shame there is nothing there!" It got a reaction in spades!!!

He sort of snarled something, jerked his pants way up, and stalked out of the store muttering obscenities. All the while, the other two guys were cracking up in wild laughter. Advantage, Garry! Of course, I could have been fired!

The second incident also happened one evening when I was working late. It did not end well. The grocery door was quiet, and I was looking down toward the registers looking for abandoned shopping carts and just watching customers in several lanes checking out. I noticed a cart near the two open lanes. A lady exiting the store was visibly upset and told me she didn't want to shop in a place with men with their pants down. A young woman was checking out at the middle register, and her boyfriend was leaning on a shopping cart pushed up against the shopping bag carousel. He had one leg way forward, and the other leg drawn way back. His back was sort of arched with his rear end stuck way out in the exit aisle in front of the registers. He had on jeans with no belt, and bright red and green under shorts. His jeans were low enough that I could see a little of his bare leg below his shorts. He was clearly enjoying showing everyone his uncovered rear end, and all the time, he was carrying on a loud conversation with his girlfriend.

Women were checking out on both sides of the register where he and his girlfriend were checking out. Everyone was growing more uncomfortable by the minute. A Walmart manager was nowhere to be seen.

I am not sure they would have taken any kind of action anyway. Right or wrong, management usually takes a more passive approach to situations unless something occurs that threatens or disrupts customer shopping. Associates are not allowed to intervene. What happened next violated that company policy. None of that was on my mind at the time. All I could see was that disgusting man's bared rear end on display for the world to see while he flexed and preened!

As I began pushing the cart away, I told him his rear end was exposed. As I walked away, I heard his girlfriend say, "What did he say to you?" I turned, and said, "His pants are too low!" I returned to the grocery entrance door and put the cart away.

Shortly after I put the cart away, the man I had confronted approached me and began cursing me, and told me that it was none of my "f....g" business how he wore his pants. I told him I was sorry if I had offended him, but he had offended other people in the store. He told me to "f..k" myself, and demanded to speak to a manager. I sent him to customer service. When he left the store, he flipped me off, and told me to "f..k" myself.

Later, the team lead in charge of the front end that night called me into her office and asked me what had happened. She then asked me to make a written report.

The next day, I was met by a coach, and taken to the "BIG" office, the office of the store manager. He was waiting for us, and a cover was placed over the office door window, not a good sign.

I was told to have a seat and tell my side of the story from last night's incident. When I finished, he reminded me that I did not have the authority to call out any customer for any reason, and that I should have called a coach.

I told him I completely understood, but that the customer would have been gone by the time any manager got to the front end. The customer that complained about the man's behavior was so upset, I assumed authority I did not have. I told him the incident was so offensive, I would probably handle it the same way if it happened again!

A first warning was placed in my file and remained there for one year. Three "coachings" in one year can lead to dismissal.

The third incident was much less controversial, and kind of funny. A young man entered the store with his pants sagging. He was barely able to walk. As he passed me, I told him I was writing a book with a chapter about sagging pants. I asked him if he could help me understand the custom. He smirked and sped up. Speed and waddle do not work well together.

I quickly grabbed my cell phone and pretended to be taking his picture (absolutely not allowed) as I called out to him that I would just use the picture. NO picture was taken! I am dumb, but not stupid!

Mission accomplished! Those pants were QUICKLY pulled up! A boring morning had just become more fun! Thank God nobody was watching the cameras that morning.

As I finish this chapter, I still do not understand this practice. Women seem to be disgusted by it, but they defend it when you intervene. It offends many shoppers, but Walmart prefers to leave things as they are.

Someday, I suspect it will take its place with ducktails and all the rest! It can't happen too soon!

The Devil Made Me Do It!

It was Thursday, and we were right in the middle of the Covid pandemic. I would be going home in about forty minutes. I was really tired. I couldn't stand trash at the front of the store, so I was sweeping up litter in my spare time when I looked up and noticed this forty to fifty year-old man trying to go under the tape barrier. Customers were only allowed to enter through one door, and only so many customers could be in the store at any one time. It was nerve wrecking! There were three of us associates at the Grocery door. We were up to our necks in all kinds of Covid rules and regulations. He had come from the handicapped parking area where he had parked his truck. He stumbled and fell twice, but finally made it. He could have walked an additional ten feet and avoided all this stupidity. He had already been told to go to the end of the barricade to enter properly. People get injured when we let them do stupid things! We are responsible! I was frustrated, so I hollered, "It probably would have been smarter to walk an additional ten feet and come in the RIGHT way."

He turned around and glared at me. Then he shouted, "Go to hell you f___ing old man!" In a nanosecond, I felt older and more tired at that moment than any day I can remember. Maybe it was the timing. Maybe it was because I had just stood at the grave of a dear friend who died way too soon just the previous week. Maybe it was because I have spent an entire life practicing positive thinking, and I was not being very positive. While I was trying to process all those feelings and emotions, I heard him shout at the other two associates at the entrance, "Tell that old man to shut the f___k up! I snapped! I took off across the parking lot and stomped up and around the barricade. When I got to the doors, I threw the dustpan and broom against the wall, and charged through the double door. I heard one of my fellow associates holler, "DON'T, Garry! Don't get fired!" Uncontrollable rage was in control, and I charged through the inner doors to see him on an electric cart ignoring another rule and going the wrong way on the exit side in front of people trying to leave the store, totally ignoring social separation. When he saw me, he gave me the finger and shouted "F___k off, old man!" People stopped and stared.

God kind of took over in that moment! Common sense and self-control took over, and I watched as he drove off into the store. He was rude and inconsiderate to anyone in his path. He simply was not worth losing my job, and I realized that finally. ANY kind of confrontation with him would have had a bad ending.

This kind of experience with rude people happens way too frequently in Walmart. Management takes a passive "live and let live" approach to these kinds of episodes, and associates are expected to suck it up and just take it. The customer is always right! I disagree, but I don't get to make the rules. In the new car dealerships I managed or owned, this man would have been thrown out of the store! Foul language and rude behavior were not tolerated. We would have called the offender out, and if the behavior didn't change, they would be told to leave the premises! GOOD customers and loyal employees were NEVER sacrificed to appease a jerk! EVERY store I managed or owned was in the top one percent in sales AND customer satisfaction in the United States, so I KNOW our success formula worked.

I returned to the front doors much to the relief of my two fellow associates, and we tried to return to normal...except it wasn't normal. You can't just turn a switch when something like that happens. There is anger and frustration and hurt. Work is not fun anymore. It is an opportunity for God to do His best work! I remember slipping away for a few minutes, and just praying for God to get me past these moments...to help me understand and go on. In a few minutes,

I was feeling much better about myself and others. All the NICE people coming into the store made a big difference too. Smiles matter! Courtesy matters!

Then he left! He rode the electric card out to his truck to transport the one tiny purchase he had made, ignoring the sign on the cart forbidding customers from taking it outside. He left it in a handicapped parking space blocking a whole parking space, and left. Except he DIDN'T leave. He drove down to the exit, and then circled back one last time past the grocery door entrance. As he drove by, he gave the one finger salute one last time and shouted more obscenities. This was all accomplished while he was driving at least ten miles faster than traffic allowed. He was just a jerk. He was also a coward!

But alas! Vengeance is mine saith the Lord! Or maybe, it is just mine! It was Saturday evening, just three days later, and he was back! He marched into the store and demanded an electric cart. Since they were all in use, we told him he must wait if he was to have one. He dragged a chair out of the Subway restaurant adjacent to the grocery entrance and squatted on it almost in the pathway of everyone coming into the store, and just glared. He glared at us. He glared at customers. He glared at LIFE! He was just a very unhappy man! It was a little after 6 PM.

Enter the little demon into the tiny recesses of my mind! Every time a cart was turned in, we took it to the other doors for a "waiting" customer. I intercepted one waiting customer as she was leaving the checkout area. I hurriedly told her about some of the things this man had done and asked her to use the other exit. I explained that I was violating Walmart policy, but she laughed out loud and said, "This is fun!" I smiled under my mask! This WAS fun! I was feeling quite a bit better! The little demon was kicking butt!

Finally, it was time to clock out and go home, and he was still sitting and glaring. It was almost seven, and Walmart lets us clock out at 6:51, nine minutes early. I clocked out and went to the back of the store to pick up a couple grocery items we needed at home. As I headed back up front, I saw him going around the corner on an electric cart. He had finally managed to get one on his own. As I was checking out at the self-check out by the pharmacy, I saw him in an angry argument with three pharmacy associates as the metal curtain closed behind them. He was too late to make his purchases even though he could easily have WALKED the few hundred feet from his chair ANY time in the last hour and gotten there before closing. It was a shorter walk than where he had parked, or he could even have parked in a special designated place, and we would have brought his prescription to his truck.

As I finished my purchases, he was still yelling and swearing, and the three associates turned and walked away. I exited the store. The little demon was dancing and turning cartwheels as I passed him and smiled.

There is a postlude to this story. I am a Christian, and I had given in to my darker side. My conscience was having a field day! That's how God works!

Over the next few days, I was overcome by guilt. I knew that this wrong had to be fixed if I was to have inner peace. God was not giving me any wiggle room!

Most of my co-workers knew of my little war on nasty. A couple had even been accomplices, keeping me posted when Mr. Evil was showing up. I told all of them that I had taken this too far and wanted to fix it the next time he visited the store.

My opportunity came a few days later. He was sitting on the stool I sometimes use, and he had positioned himself right in the middle of the grocery store aisle in a place where he could watch inside the store and also see down the exit aisle in front of the checkout registers.

This was where he would wait while he waited for an electric cart to show up, and he would glare at everyone passing by.

I quickly checked and found out we had an electric cart at the other entrance. I remember silently confessing to God that I really didn't like this guy. I prayed to God, "Change my heart! Let this man see You, dear Lord, through me! Keep me calm and focused, Lord! I'm nervous, Lord! Don't let me screw this up!" And I was off!

He was looking away as I approached and didn't see me until I was twenty or thirty feet from him. The snarl and glare was instantaneous! I saw the "F" word forming on his lips!

He didn't get the chance! I closed the distance quickly and put on the biggest smile I could muster while extending my hand. "Sir, we have an electric cart at the other door, and an associate is bringing it to you right now!"

He was glaring at me, but now there was also a look of confusion. Mr. Evil seemed just a little less evil! I knew I had to send a strong signal that whatever was between us was now behind us. God expected it!

He finally reached out and gripped my extended hand in a limp and lukewarm handshake. As we shook hands, some of the tension that seemed to always be controlling him softened.

As the electric cart was about to arrive, I quickly told him, "It's time we put our differences behind us. I am sorry for any bad things that have happened between us. Let's go forward! Welcome to Walmart! Look me up the next time you come to Walmart, and I will make sure we find you an electric cart."

Mr. Evil had just left the building. In his place was a man who was a little less angry and bitter than he had been just a few moments before. Standing beside him was a Walmart Customer Host/Greeter feeling a little better now that the burden had just been lifted from his shoulders.

I got what could be called a VERY WEAK smile as he mumbled, "Thanks". It wasn't much, but the war was over. The devil made me do it, but God won!

Sherita

Walmart is a huge, gargantuan corporation that is spread around the world, generating almost 800 billion dollars in sales every year. It dwarfs its competition. It now employs 2,300,000 associates. It's BIG! It serves over 230,000,000 customers.

The store where I work in Sikeston, Missouri covers over 230,000 square ft. Last year, the store had almost $120,000,000 in sales. About 350 full- and part-time associates work here. Every day, thousands of customers shop here, depending on the weather and time of the year. The first day of every month is a madhouse, as customers who receive food stamps or government benefits flood the store. Holidays and special occasions like Christmas, Valentine's Day, Easter, Memorial Day, Mothers and Fathers Days, July 4th, Back-to-School start up, Labor Day, Halloween, Thanksgiving are all retail opportunities for special promotions.

All of these occasions, along with the population's daily needs, feed a constant stream of customers through our doors. A contracted worker recently making adjustments to our grocery entrance doors, told me that approximately 23 million customers have been through those doors since the store was built in the early 2000s.

Welcome to Walmart! We are busy! All that traffic creates a lot of emotions and reactions from customers AND associates. Shopping can be stressful when we are surrounded by crying babies, children with too much energy, rude customers, unattended shopping carts left everywhere, electric carts moving through the aisles, associates pushing huge carts as they shop for our grocery pick up customers, confused senior citizens as they try to figure out where everything is, vendors and associates trying to keep the shelves stocked. There's a lot going on ALL the time!

ALL of this makes me think of Sherita! Sherita is a pretty, petite African American woman in her 40s. I don't believe I have ever seen her when she wasn't smiling. Or at least had a pleasant look on her face. She's normal. She's human! She can get angry or upset or hurt, but she always manages to mask it with that beautiful smile that just warms up a room!

Sometimes, I enjoy just watching her from a distance as she does her job. She is one of the shoppers in the grocery pick-up department, so she is constantly going all over the store as she fills customer orders. These shoppers are timed. They are graded on the time it takes to complete an order, so there is stress. There is pressure.

This is not a problem for Sherita. If she sees a frustrated customer who can't find something, she will stop, and flash that beautiful smile. In a millisecond, the customer has his or her answer, and is cheerfully on their way. That is because Sherita is a superb listener, and in the midst of a pressure packed busy day, she has just completely paused her crazy schedule, and made that customer the most important person in the store!!!

I've been in management my entire professional life until I went to work for Walmart. I have managed lots of employees. The customer was royalty! That was my standard for excellence. EVERYTHING evolved around that fundamental principle.

Over the course of my career, I witnessed some employees that immediately "got it", and some employees that had to be constantly reminded or pushed to a higher standard. And then there were those employees that just didn't care. No matter how hard we worked with them or retrained them, they just would not put forth the extra effort. I never tolerated that kind of job performance very long.

Walmart has all of these types in their stores. The labor market is tight, and, sometimes, Walmart settles for people that would never have made the grade in my companies.

But Sherita is a grade above ALL of these people! Walmart would do well to CLONE her if they could! As a person who has spent my entire professional life hiring and managing people, until I came to Walmart, it is just a joy to watch this young woman in action as she performs her job, and SO MUCH MORE!!!

She takes great pride in organizing her work. She works in the outside grocery pickup department, so she is an in-store shopper filling customer orders. She is one of 74,000 associates dedicated to shopping for others. These orders can take a shopper all over a store. A Walmart Supercenter stocks an average of over 145,000 items. Our store has approximately 230,000 square feet. That's a LOT of territory to cover while you are filling an order and being timed for efficiency. Time and store knowledge are important. Each shopper has a small handheld computer scanner or company furnished smart phone to help them navigate and locate items.

Sherita has an uncanny knowledge of store products. She fills orders quickly because she KNOWS where the item is located and doesn't have to use precious time on the scanner or phone. She manages to do this while smiling at everyone she meets, constantly assisting frustrated customers or other associate shoppers locate an elusive product. Sometimes, she will just leave her shopping cart for a minute and walk the customer to the product. Of course, this is always done with a smile that lights up the store, and a bubbly conversation that leaves the customer beaming with appreciation and gratitude that someone in this crazy busy world cares!

Recently, as she was finished for the day, checking out in the self-check area, I observed her having this animated conversation with one of our young customers. I know this young lady professionally. She is a teller in one of our local banks. The two of them were laughing and carrying on and babbling about just about everything…kids, God, work, the weather, bla, bla, bla!!! I finally walked over and asked how they knew each other. Sherita just laughed and said they didn't really know each other. They had just met and connected while one stocked and the other shopped! A few minutes later they both walked out of the store together talking about some of life's challenges, and how we just have to turn it all over to God!!!

Both of these women are valuable assets to their employers. They both care about others. They both have a strong faith and are not afraid to share it. They both are great parents. They teach their kids the same values that guide their lives. They both check life's challenges at the door when they come to work. They are positive in their actions and their interactions. Their glass of life is never empty, or even half empty. It is always full or filling up!!!

I visited with Sherita recently and asked her about the people and events that had shaped her life. She was uncomfortable about talking about herself. She admitted that she moved in a small circle of friends in school. When I pressed her, she admitted that her grandmother had impacted her the most, instilling many of the values I see in her as she goes about her daily duties.

Then she got kind of quiet and reflective. She confessed that sometimes life had been very hard for her. She admitted that people sometimes hurt her, but she never allowed those feelings to be exposed. "I pray! I go God and let God!" "I have anger issues. That doesn't mean that I am an angry person, but, sometimes, people make me angry when they are mean or nasty or hurtful. I just have to turn it over to God!" As she said these things, her face and composure changed from sad and reflective to bright and happy! You could see that instant transformation that God had accomplished right there in the middle of our conversation! Sherita, without even realizing it, had just shared the secret that makes strangers love her!

Does God make us a better employee? I think the answer is a little more complex. God makes us a better PERSON! Life throws lots of curves in our path. Some of those curves can turn us upside down in the blink of an eye. It may be an illness. It may be the loss of someone we love. We may be a bullying victim. It may be a chance encounter with an angry stranger in our path, maybe in the aisle at Walmart. It may be a financial disaster. It may be a broken relationship, a bitter divorce. It may be ANYTHING! Life is cruel sometimes. Life can completely knock us down sometimes. In my darkest hours my friends would tell me that God never gives us more than we can handle. I do not believe that. There were MANY times when I simply could not handle it. I learned that God never gave me more than GOD could handle!

"Go God! Let God!" I realized, as I stood there and listened to Sherita share this very personal secret to her inner happiness, that I was hearing a testimony that can change a life when we finally realize we are never alone. She and I had arrived at the same place through completely different paths, but God had found both of us in our journeys, just like He can rescue anybody when they discover this amazing simple truth!

Thank you, Sherita! Thank you for your smile! Thank you for your positive energy! Thank you for your faith! Thank you for your example! You make me a better person! You make Walmart a better place! You make our world a better place! Thanks for making a difference!

As this book goes to press, I am happy to report that Sherita is now a team lead in her department. Thank you, Walmart for recognizing your "spark" in others!

Those Service Animals

Their names were Bubba and Biggie Smalls. One was called a "puggle", and the other was a Victorian Bulldog. Both had the familiar harness with "Service Animal" in large bold letters down both sides of their harnesses.

Their mistress and master each held onto a large leash controlling the animals. When Bubba entered Walmart, he was snuggled on a blanket and riding in a shopping cart. Biggie Smalls walked quietly beside his master.

They entered Walmart on different days and had no connection to each other. Neither dog looked like they needed to be secured by a leash, but State law requires it for the safety of others.

I have seen hundreds of service animals enter Walmart. Most are dogs, but I have also seen cats, monkeys, a hamster, and one snake! The snake may have been an impostor! The snake and the monkey came into the other entrance. I would have called a manager before allowing them into the store, but it's Walmart!!!

Service animals are welcome at Walmart. Pets are not allowed. That rule is pretty much universally ignored. Every day, we have many household pets enter our doors. When we challenge them, most of the owners claim they are service animals. Management does not allow us to take the matter any further even though many of the animals are NOT service animals.

One time, I confronted an off-duty associate pushing a cart with FIVE baby puppies roaming all over her groceries inside her cart. They were less than ten days old and definitely not potty trained.

She informed me they were ALL service dogs! You can't make this stuff up!

All of these legitimate service animals have stories. When I asked Bubba's owner if she was comfortable discussing her situation with me, I explained that I was writing a book about people that come to Walmart, and it might enlighten some of our readers.

She nodded her head and then lowered her eyes. In a very soft voice, she whispered, "Cancer". Her mother, who was behind her and her dog, was starting to tear up. I was feeling a little bad about asking her about her situation, but she quickly shook her head. She told me it was okay, and she was glad to share her story.

I thanked her and told her that I was grateful that she had a companion that loved her and was there to support her through her journey. I let her know that she and her family would be in my prayers. We talked a little bit about the progress that was being made every day in cancer research. As we talked, I noticed her mother standing quietly behind her trying hard to control her emotions and not start crying.

I was reminded that for most of us, cancer is a nasty word that generates memories of someone we love or knew that fought cancer, but for this woman, she was living the experience right before my eyes! This was her daughter who was supposed to outlive her! This was her daughter whom she had raised from childhood. All of that was in doubt now, as her daughter was battling this dreadful disease while all she could do was painfully watch.

As all this was happening, Bubba just sat there, patiently waiting for his mistress. As she talked to me, she began to pet him, stroking the top of his head. Dog and mistress looked into each other's eyes lovingly as she let me look a little bit into her soul. She talked about how much Bubba lifted her spirits. She talked about how the doctors and nurses petted him when she went for her treatments. All this time she was gently petting him, and he was just sleepily looking up at her with those big loving eyes.

As they went on into the store, you could just see the peace this Bubba was bringing to this daughter and mother. I give thanks for Bubba!!!

Biggie Smalls is a completely different kind of story with the same result. Biggie Smalls and his master came into the store several times before we talked. This dog is beautiful with spectacular markings that I had never seen on a dog before. I was not familiar with the breed.

My research tells me they are a cross between English Bulldogs, Bull Terriers, Bull Mastiffs, and Staffordshire Bull Terriers. The sole purpose of the breed was to create a healthier Bulldog, which was a major success.

Biggie Smalls was CERTAINLY the picture of good health as he walked proudly and quietly beside his master, and he was an instant celebrity every time they came into the store. EVERYBODY noticed him, and most people could be seen to say something. Some would pet him as his master beamed.

When I finally got a chance to chat with his owner one day, I asked him if he was comfortable sharing a little about Biggie Small, and the reason he had him. I explained that I was writing this book about people who had come into Walmart, and I asked him why he had a service dog.

He paused, and looked at me, and said, "I hate people!" Whoa!!! That will slow down a conversation!

Then, he flashed this great big, beautiful smile, and he said, "Not anymore! Biggie Smalls has changed all of that! After I got him, and we would go out in public together, everybody loved him, and he loved everybody. It made me very uncomfortable. I didn't much like being around people very much, but everybody just loved that dog! He wouldn't let me keep hating them!" Then, he laughed out loud, and scratched Biggie Smalls' head, and Biggie Smalls licked his hand. Dog and master were feeling good!

As they left the store, I tried to process what I had just witnessed. He was a man with deep psychological issues. I have no idea whether he had received or was receiving counseling. We did not discuss faith or God, but it was obvious that this beautiful Victorian Bulldog had been a bridge back to a more normal relationship with other people. That is pretty profound!

Recently, a young woman entered our store with her service dog following her mother. While they were reviewing their shopping list, I explained about my book, and asked the young woman if she would feel comfortable talking about her service animal. Both daughter and mother enthusiastically responded. They seemed eager to teach a stranger!

We began by exchanging names and a little background information on the dog. The young woman's name was Sharina, and she assured me it was okay using her real name when I wrote about her story. The dog's name was Xander. She was a full bred Labrador Retriever, and she was absolutely beautiful. Her reddish hair glistened in the store's light!

I learned that Xander was seven years old, and Sharina had gotten her when she was five. Sharina told me she was legally blind and suffered from a rare disease that had stolen her eyesight when she was very young. When I asked her what had changed for her since she and Xander became a team, she flashed a beautiful smile, and proclaimed, "She has given me independence!"

But lots would happen in young Xander"s life before she and Sharina would meet for the first time.

Xander was her first service dog. She had come from The Seeing Eye, Inc., a guide dog school located in Morris Township, New Jersey. The school was founded in 1929 and is the oldest guide dog school in the country. It is also one of the largest.

Puppies begin their training when they are seven to eight weeks old. Volunteer puppy raisers will foster these puppies and begin their basic training. The training is very structured, and the puppy raiser is responsible for exposing the young animal to different environments, all kinds of people and animals, anything else they might encounter The dog learns basic commands like sit, rest, down, come, basic house manners, walking on a leash ahead and on the handler's left side with little distraction.

These puppies attend monthly meetings and interact with other puppies in training. In this environment, they will interact with other dogs, and children, and anything else they might encounter once they are assigned.

At thirteen to nineteen months, the dogs are returned to The Seeing Eye. They spend a month getting health screenings, are neutered or spayed, and given a dental cleaning.

Each dog is then assigned to a dedicated trainer with whom they will train for four months. They are regularly trained in a variety of rural, suburban, and urban environments culminating in a trip to New York City.

Dogs are taught to guide with a combination of repetition and praise. Clicker training enhances the dog's skill in targeting specific objects. Halfway through training, instructors take a blindfolded tour to test the dog's abilities. A more complicated blindfolded course takes place at the end of their training to make sure the dog is ready to begin work with their new owners.

A class then follows for the dogs and their new owners that lasts for about a month. During this time, the dogs must form a bond with their new handler. The handlers must be sixteen or older.

The Seeing Eye, Inc. is a 501(c)(3) non-profit organization, funded by donations from individuals, foundations, and corporations. Their students have all paid the same nominal fee since the 1930s.

All of the above information about training was obtained from the Seeing Eye Inc. website. According to Guiding Eyes.org, it can cost up to $50,000 annually to train and care for a guide dog throughout its working lifetime with a person who is blind.

My encounters with these three amazing dogs, and the people they were serving, has opened my eyes to a world that most of us don't know, or even understand. I see dozens of pets enter the store where I work every day. The real service animals are easy to spot. They all are indifferent to everything around them except for their master or mistress. They are extremely well behaved. They never make messes while in the store. The people they serve are living better lives because they are there.

The pet owners that pretend their pets are service animals give the program a bad name. Most of these animals clearly do not belong in any store. But until Walmart toughens its enforcement, I don't see many changes.

It doesn't matter to me anymore. The difference these amazing service animals make is reason enough for me to look past the others. Give yourself a treat the next time you encounter an animal with that familiar distinctive harness. It might just change your life!

The Bird Lady

One morning I was walking across the Walmart parking lot, and as I got to the handicapped parking area, I noticed large amounts of bird seed spread out over much of the parking lot. Hundreds of small birds were gobbling the food, fluttering a few feet away as customers came and went, and then they would quickly return and gorge themselves on all this bird seed someone had left for them.

Shopping carts were standing randomly about the parking area where customers had left them, and birds were perched on them, letting their droppings drip down in the carts. NOT GOOD!!! Thus began one of the strangest things I have ever seen at Walmart!

I went inside and found my manager. She gave me permission to go out and clean up the mess. It took over forty-five minutes to get all the bird seed swept up. The birds quickly left when their food supply was gone. I returned to my job at the front door, and thought the problem was behind us. I should have known better! It's Walmart!

The next day, the handicap parking area was covered again with bird seed. I estimated at least three bags. At ten dollars to twenty dollars a bag, this was costing someone some serious money!

Birds can be filthy animals. They can carry all kinds of parasites. They can transfer diseases. I didn't want them feasting in our parking lot! I didn't want them pooping on any more carts!

It didn't seem to matter. Every morning, there was more birdseed. The bird lover seemed to be driven by some weird undefined passion. On day four, I noticed two areas some distance apart. Birdseed was still being spread throughout handicapped parking, but now I found a bag or two of birdseed spread around one of our cart bays. Hundreds of birds were feeding around the cart bay, and then perching all over the carts while they let their droppings fall at will all over the parked carts.

This was not only disgusting, but also unsanitary, and downright dangerous! I went straight to the asset protection office and delivered the news to the asset protection manager, and reminded her that Walmart could be held liable if anything bad happened to a customer, and traced back to one of those carts.

Management was now in agreement that something had to be done. We have cameras covering the entire parking lot. Asset protection promised to review videos of the parking lot and try to identify the guilty party.

The next morning, bird seed was back on the parking lot in the same two areas. I went straight to asset protection and confronted the manager. She told me the culprit had been identified, and the matter was being handled. She could not reveal any more details.

I found out later that the guilty party was a lady working at Walmart on our night shift. She just felt bad for all the hungry birds out there, and decided it was her responsibility to do something about it. I was told she hadn't considered the health dangers she might be creating by her misdirected concern for the birds. In a little less than a week, she had spent about $300 to $400 on birdseed!

She was called in and promised to stop feeding the birds. I guess the birds flew back to the fields where they came from. Shake my head! It's Walmart!

Wanda

I WAS BUSY PUTTING AWAY SOME STRAY CARTS WHEN HER CAREGIVER brought her into the store. She was sitting in a wheelchair, and her caregiver pushed her inside the grocery entrance and then went to park her car.

Wanda was just sitting in her wheelchair, slumped over, looking very alone. One shoulder was noticeably much lower than the other, and she was sort of just staring down into her lap.

I felt compelled to go over and speak to her. She didn't seem to notice me until I was standing beside her and spoke, "Good morning! Welcome to Walmart! We are glad you are here!"

That got a feeble response, and a twisted smile that was one of the most beautiful things I saw that day! It was the eyes that pushed it over the top! Those eyes were trying so hard to let me look into this woman's heart!

She had obviously suffered a serious stroke. All the signs were there. Confusion, and lack of awareness, the drooping mouth, the slumping shoulder, and the clutched hand. And yet there she was, fighting through all she had been through, trying to look up at me and showing me her inner strength and determination!

I gave her a big hug, and told her, "You are the most beautiful gift that God has brought me today!" She beamed as her caregiver came in, and introduced us.

"This is Wanda!" she said with a smile, and Wanda's smile got bigger! I told them to enjoy their shopping, and thanked them again for making my day more special!

About two hours later, I saw them checking out. Wanda was already smiling that crooked smile as her caregiver pushed her my way. As they went past, I got one last hug, and a promise to be back soon. The caregiver was doing most of the talking. Wanda was struggling to put sentences together, and finding words. It didn't matter. Everyone knew what she was trying to say. Going shopping at Walmart had brought a little sunshine into a life made darker by a devastating stroke. Promises were made to be back soon, and they pushed out the door.

That's how I met Wanda!

I've seen Wanda many times since that day. She would show up every week or two. I began to notice subtle improvements in her ability to control body movements, and she seemed to be more alert. She began to sit more erect.

One thing did not change. That smile was always there every time I would greet her! Those eyes were just as bright and piercing.

She was definitely improving right before my eyes. Her speech was better. She was forming complete sentences without stumbling. It seemed that we would always share some little tidbit about each other almost every time she visited the store.

One day, the local Sikeston Transit Authority van pulled up, and the driver came around and opened the side door. There sat Wanda in her wheel chair, making her first trip to Walmart by herself since her stroke!

We celebrated with a high five when she entered the store. Using her good hand, she laughed out loud as she slapped my hand!

I turned around, and faced inside the store. In a loud voice, I hollered, "WANDA IS ENTERING THE BUILDING!" Several of the cashiers who had gotten to know her cheered and clapped. Wanda rolled her wheel chair forward into the store using her good hand. Several customers turned and smiled as they knew something special was happening.

The look on Wanda's face, and that beautiful smile took on a glow that brightened the whole grocery entrance! There was a lump in my throat as I watched her proudly enter the store all by herself, shopping bags hanging from the handle bars on the back of the chair.

When she was ready to check out, it took her some time, but she managed to reach around behind the wheel chair into the shopping bags, always using her good hand and arm, and get out every one of her purchases by herself. She then got out her card, and paid.

She was noticeably tired, but as she rolled out of the grocery self-check, there was a look of quiet pride as she celebrated her accomplishment! Here was this young woman who could not even hold her head up a few months earlier, and she had just come to Walmart, and gone shopping all by herself!

I got another big high five when she was ready for her ride! As the van pulled away, I quietly thanked God for my friend, Wanda!

After that day, I would see improvements in her social skills and her speech and her energy every time she came in. I thanked God over and over for surrounding her with that love and peace that surpasses our human understanding. Sometimes, we would talk about our faith. She became an inspiration to all of us who had gotten to know her.

I will never forget that day when I was watching the self-check area with my back momentarily to the door. There was this soft tap on my left shoulder. I turned around, and there was Wanda! Her wheel chair was a few feet behind her. She had stood up, and walked the six or eight feet up behind me.

I turned completely around, and was just too choked up to say anything. We wrapped our arms around each other, and just stood there hugging each other tightly as the tears rolled down our cheeks.

She still comes into the store regularly. She continues to use the wheel chair. Walking that day was her special gift to me! Only God knows whether she will be able to push it aside some day, but she continues to inspire everyone who crosses her path!

When Nelia, my second wife, had her devastating stroke, Wanda found out. One day, after Nelia had gotten out of the hospital, and was well enough to get out, we loaded up and went to Walmart. We managed to run into Wanda.

Wanda rolled her wheel chair over close to Nelia's wheel chair and reached out and took Nelia's good hand. Nelia had lost the ability to talk when she had her stroke, but as Wanda continued to hold her hand, Wanda looked over at her with those beautiful piercing eyes, and spoke quietly to her. The words of hope and encouragement were just pouring out of Wanda's mouth.

Nelia began to cry softly, and then she made this little bubbly noise as she was trying so hard to form words she no longer knew. Wanda and Nelia had entered some special holy place. Nelia was tightly squeezing Wanda's hand now! The tears had turned to laughter. Two women who had been in the same dark place were now bringing light to each other.

As these two women bonded, I quietly thanked God for bringing us all together at Walmart that afternoon!

Nelia's stroke was much worse than Wanda's, and she never got stronger after those first few months. Eleven months after her stroke, she developed an infection that turned septic. It took her life a few days later.

Those were hard days. Work was not easy. Wanda always found me, and she always cheered me up. This woman who has been through so much, whose life has been permanently changed by the stroke that ravaged her, always finds a way to bring a little sunshine to others.

I am pretty sure there are some angel wings tucked away in that wheel chair somewhere! Thank you, Wanda, for making our world a better place!

The Man With No Pants!

I suppose it was bound to happen someday! After all, it IS Walmart! I just wasn't ready for that. I'm not sure you are ever ready for that!

The day started normally enough. I saw him when I first arrived for work at nine o'clock. He was a Vietnam veteran about seventy years old. I have seen him before. He drives an older silver blue Mercury Grand Marquis with minor to moderate body damage on all four quarters. He always parks in handicap parking, and he's not above telling someone else to move! He is a chain smoker, and lives out of his car. The car is stuffed with his personal possessions and clothes. The floorboards are stuffed with napkins and torn paper towels. Most of them have been used. The car reeks of tobacco.

He DEMANDS that we bring electric carts out to his car, even though he is able to walk. He will usually recruit an associate or customer to unload his cart, and then he will practically always chew them out for not putting everything exactly where he wants it in the car! He is a dirty, nasty and MEAN old man!

I have thanked him for his service, and he tells me to go to Hell! I have welcomed him to Walmart, and he tells me to get the hell out of his way! I have heard him get mad at a customer for not bringing him the electric cart he wanted! He is a dirty, nasty and MEAN old man!!!!

He came into the store finally after badgering a customer to bring him an electric cart. He sat on the cart beside his car for about thirty minutes just smoking and making a mess in the parking lot. Then he slowly came across the parking lot and parked in front of the building where he proceeded to chain smoke and make a new mess.

Finally, he drove the cart into the building without a mask even though they were required at the time because of the Covid-19. He managed to stay inside for about two hours, and then he exited and headed back to his car. He sat on the cart and smoked until a customer walked by. He told the customer he needed help loading the two small bags of merchandise he had purchased into his car. Then, he asked the customer to help him into his car even though he had exited his car earlier by himself and walked to the cart!

This saga soon required the help of a SECOND customer. Finally, they got him transferred. When they entered the store, they were muttering about how rude he was.

I guess that wore him out, because he just sat there in his parking spot chain smoking for another thirty or forty minutes. Finally, he started his car and drove slowly to the east end of the parking lot where he parked under two big trees, and spent the next four hours there chain smoking and making a nice big mess beside his car.

I saw him driving toward the exits, and thought we were through with him for the day! I shouldn't have started celebrating. He got to the last aisle and made a right turn back toward the store. He drove to the end of the aisle and made another right turn back toward me. He slowly drove past the grocery entrance and proceeded to park in one of two long handicap parking spaces provided for long trucks or campers. I guess that was appropriate because he later decided to camp there, but not yet! He had to upset a few more associates and customers first!

He cornered a young high school student who had just started as a part-time cart pusher the previous week. Someone had left an electric cart outside, and the young man was bringing it into the store. The old man hollered at him to bring it to him. But he wasn't through. He had to get the poor kid to help him on the cart. Then he sat on it and chained smoked before finally entering the store.

He exited about thirty minutes later with a small bag of purchases, and rode the cart out to his car. He had been miraculously healed while shopping, because he lit up a new cigarette, and threw the old one on the parking lot. Then, he climbed off the cart and walked the short distance to his car, and climbed inside with no assistance.

I breathed a sigh of relief to finally be rid of him, or so I thought! Stupid me!

Instead of leaving, he finished his cigarette and opened the driver door. The next time I looked up, I saw two bony white legs sticking out the door with just a corner of red and green boxer shorts. While I was still trying to take all of that in, the boxer shorts came all the way down and off, and he promptly threw them into the back seat. Then, he whipped out another pair that I presume were clean, and proceeded to put THEM on. He pulled them to his knees, and then stood up outside the car bare butt naked from the waist down, and slowly pulled them up. He then leisurely climbed back in the car.

Customers were scattering! Several complained as they entered. While all of this was going on, he proceeded to find a hospital urinal somewhere in the depths of all that mess inside the car. Just when I thought things could not get any worse, he planted both stocking covered feet on the pavement, pushed the urinal between his legs, and relieved himself. When he was through, he poured the contents of the urinal out on the pavement beside his car, put the urinal away somewhere in the car, put the driver seat in a reclining position, stuck his bare legs out the open driver's door and through the open window...sitting in just his undershorts.

He was chain smoking the entire time, and the cigarette butts were piling up outside the car.

Management had been called, but nobody had come up. I walked to the customer service desk and was told to call the police. It was nearly time for me to leave for the day, but I called on my cell phone.

Ten minutes later a young police officer arrived, and parked behind the old man's car. The door was still open, and his feet were still sticking out the window. He was still sitting there in just his boxer shorts. The young officer just began conversing with him, but they were too far away to make out what was being said.

I had done my job! After a few minutes, I went ahead and clocked out. As I drove out of the parking lot, the conversation was continuing....

Wally

Dogs are man's best friend, at least that's what I've always been told. We always had dogs on our family farm in Western Kansas. I remember so many good times playing with them.

There was Big Ben, a pure bred collie that was one of the smartest dogs I've ever been around. We would take walks with him to round up the milk cows grazing in the pasture. Back on the family farm, when one of the cows would stray, Big Ben would take off and circle around them. He would stand in their path, and bark until they would turn back. He would trot behind them, and rejoin us when they were back in the herd.

We walked the one and one-quarter mile to the little one room Northstar School where I attended through the eighth grade. He would always walk us to the end of the driveway, and lay down and watch us as we headed out. He would be waiting when we came home, jumping up on us and licking our faces, then walking beside us to the house.

I don't know what he did during the day, but he was always there every day. We all loved Big Ben!

There was little Penny. She was a mixed breed terrier. She became part of our family one day when my parents, my younger brother and I visited some friends of theirs who lived in Ulysses, Kansas. Larry and I played with that little dog all afternoon. It was an instant love affair! When it was time to leave, the couple surprised us and offered to let us take Penny home. Larry and I went crazy! We were jumping up and down, and Penny was jumping up and down, and we were begging Mom and Dad to let us keep her.

The deal was quickly sealed, and we rode home with Penny between us in the back seat. From that day forward, boys and dog were inseparable. She and Big Ben quickly bonded, and the four of us became family. There wasn't much that we didn't do together.

At night, Big Ben had his own dog house and he stayed outside. We had twin beds, and Penny would take turns jumping from one bed to the other, but she never strayed very far from our sides.

Big Ben died in his sleep while I was in high school. We had a quiet funeral for him, and he was buried on the family farm. Penny lived until I was in college. I remember the phone call. Mom was crying, and I broke down too. So many memories flooded my mind as I remembered. Dad and Mom buried her in a small grave near Big Ben. That became sacred ground until the farm was sold. The buyers agreed to protect those graves.

There were no more dogs in my life for the next forty-five years until 2001, when Shirley and I got our first Yorkie. Her name was Zoey, and she was eight months old when we got her. I had begged Shirley for a dog for years, and she staunchly argued against it. She didn't want an animal in the house, and didn't want the responsibility of caring for one.

That all went out the window one April morning at work when a good friend showed up at the door with Zoey! She was freshly groomed, and had a cute little pink bow atop her head. The lady set her down, and she trotted over to Shirley, and hopped up on her lap. When she licked Shirley's cheek, and Shirley looked like she had just finished her favorite dish of ice cream, I KNEW I had a dog!

A few minutes later, we had a dog! That was the last day she was really nice to Shirley! She was a one-man dog, and she adored me. She was on my lap constantly. She would always come to me, and it drove Shirley crazy. She would try to pick Zoey up, and Zoey would snarl and nip at her. Shirley would push her away, and go pout, and Zoey would come and jump on my lap.

Two years later, this woman who told me I couldn't have a dog for years, told me one night that life was not fair. "Zoey didn't love her, and she deserved a dog of her own! What?!

Two days later, we were the proud owners of TWO Yorkies! Tigger II was eight weeks old when he arrived at the Warner household. You could hold him in one hand, and it was hilarious as he and Zoey met each other for the first time. Tigger wanted to play, and Zoey would jump back and stare. Tigger was instantly in charge, and that never changed.

When Shirley died, those two little dogs mourned her loss just like me, and they seemed to know when I was having an especially tough time. They would jump up on my lap, and take their place on each side of me in the recliner.

There were many nights when I would start crying, and one or both of them would climb up and lick my tears.

I started working at Walmart on October 27, 2016. I lost Zoey one month later. She suffered a massive seizure the morning before Thanksgiving. She seemed to recover after nearly two minutes of wild thrashing on the kitchen floor, and then she just laid there, panting, but seeming to be back to normal. After a few minutes, I picked her up, and carried her out to the back yard, and gently set her down. She immediately took off running across the yard…and crashed hard into the cedar fence! It was then that I sadly realized that the seizure had left her blind.

I had to get to work, so I set out some food and penned her in the kitchen in her bed. When I came home, I don't believe she had moved all day. There was another bad seizure Thanksgiving morning, and I realized that I had no choice.

The next morning, I wrapped her in a warm blanket, and drove to my veterinarian friend's clinic. I held her as she crossed over the rainbow bridge, and then tearfully drove to work. She was cremated, and her ashes will be buried with me when I die.

Tigger and I were lost and broken without Zoey. We grieved together.

Two-and-a-half years later, our small world changed dramatically when we met Wally! I don't know what his real name was before I met him. A family drove to Walmart on June 19, 2019 and tried to push him from their van in the Walmart parking lot. When that didn't work, a young woman put him on a leash and brought him into Walmart through the pharmacy and general merchandise entrance.

She walked him into the self-checkout area, removed the leash, and quickly exited the store. All of this was recorded on Walmart cameras.

This beautiful cute little palomino colored blonde dog, with this white tail that arches up and over his back, was left to wander among customers as they paid for their purchases. Asset protection was summoned, and Wally was quickly removed to the asset protection office, as the store tried to figure out what to do with him.

I visited him several times that day, and felt something going on in my heart each time. By the time I finished my work day, I had decided to give him a home if no one stepped up. When I went down to the asset protection office, I found out that one of our dog loving associates had taken him home.

I was glad and sad all at the same time! During the day, I had gone from feeling sorry for this cute little stray dog, to taking ownership of him. Then, in an instant, I found that someone else had the same idea.

The next day, I sought out the young associate who had rescued him. She told me she already had two other dogs, and wasn't sure how well they would accept him.

My heart did a silent flip flop, and I told her I would be interested in taking him if things didn't work out. She promised to call me that evening with an update.

She called right on time, and told me things were not going well! I could come get him! It was a fifteen minute drive to her home, and I fought speeding the whole way.

She had him on a leash, and was waiting outside when I arrived. After a short chat about his overall condition, dog and new master headed back home. He whined and acted sort of frightened the whole time. When we got inside my apartment, he ran all over, smelling and exploring everything! My friend had told me that he seemed housebroken, and that turned out to be the case. He never made one mess inside the house.

He and Tigger quickly bonded which was the first hurdle. Everything else was sort of unchartered water. Zoey and Tigger had both been certified registered thoroughbred Yorkies. This new dog was a mystery.

The first decision was to give him a name. "Sam" and "Wally" were both on the short list because he had been rescued at Walmart. Wally won, and it has been the perfect name!

As soon as possible, I took him to the veterinary clinic, and had my friend examine him. He looked healthy, but he was badly infected with heart worms. After getting him all his required vaccinations and heart worm treatments, we returned home. The trip had cost $650, but I really had no choice. Heart worms are fatal if you don't treat them. A month later, Dr. Steve pronounced him cured and heart worm free!

The lonely void that Tigger and I had felt since losing Zoey had finally been filled by strangers who had abandoned their pet.

Zoey and Tigger had manners. Wally was a high strung pain in the butt! He would sit up on his hind quarters, and then tear around the house like a small tornado! When he jumped up on my lap, he would sit for a minute and then explode off.

The biggest challenge was when I went outside, or when anyone visited me. He would dart out around me or them and charge out the door, and would be gone. He was also a digger. He would dig under the fence in the back yard and escape.

I would get so mad and frustrated. It was all just a fun game to Wally. We would always find him a few blocks from home. He would be playing in someone's yard, or someone would be holding him. He was super friendly to a total stranger, and would never bite anyone. They could just hold out their hand, and he would run to them.

When I would hold out MY hand, he would just sit until I got about six feet from him, and then he would take off at full speed through a couple yards, tail arched like a flag, and totally happy with himself!

This crazy game would continue until I cornered him, or a stranger would reach out, and he would run to them. When I finally would catch him, he would roll over on his back and smile at me while I fastened the leash to his collar. Damn dog!!!

This story has been repeated more times than I can remember, but in between, dog and master have become pretty good friends. As he has grown older, the escapes have been less often, and he is not quite so hyper.

I would be lying though if I did not admit that he has caused me to learn some new words that cannot be printed here. He can really get under my skin sometimes! Damn dog! I love him!

The COVID Calamity

IN THE BLINK OF AN EYE, THE WORLD CHANGED FOREVER! THE whole experience was life changing. In just a few days, the world economy ground to a halt. The greatest US economy I can ever remember evaporated overnight. You couldn't find toilet paper. Alcohol and hand sanitizer were a distant memory. Nonessential businesses were ordered closed. Schools were shut down, and kids were sent home. Churches went online, or shut down. Life was on hold!

At first, not much changed if you worked at Walmart. We were given special passes that allowed us to drive back and forth to work. Walmart was designated an essential business, so we all got up every day, and went to work pretty much like always...for a while. Then, things started getting crazy! America was waking up to a pandemic.

Sikeston, Missouri is right in the middle of the country, so we were slow to catch up with the big cities and the coastal states. New York was a long way away. Walmart shoppers in Sikeston came and went without much fanfare. Associates did their jobs, and went home until the next day. We were happy all those COVID problems were in the big cities...until they weren't!

Missouri had gotten its first case. It wasn't close to us, but you could see a change in people's faces coming into the store. Sometimes, they would ask us if anyone sick was in the store. Mothers held their children a little closer. There was chatter in the break room about whether we were safe working around so many people.

Then, things started getting a little crazy! It started with the toilet paper. People would leave with their normal purchases...and five or six large packages of toilet paper. Some would sort of hold it lovingly like they might never see toilet paper again. We had several skirmishes between customers as supplies dwindled. Two ladies got into a shouting match when one tried to remove one of four large packages from the other lady's cart. The f-word could be heard up and down the aisle! People started calling to see if we had toilet paper on the shelf. Things got REALLY tense when the signs went up limiting toilet paper purchases to one per shopper. Of course, nobody read the signs, and our poor cashiers had to be the bearers of bad news! Profanity was the order of the day! Checkout was a bad place for young children! Young mothers and church ladies got their stuff and got out! Of course, if you were at the entrances, you felt the full brunt of an irate customer's wrath.

Rubbing alcohol and hand sanitizer were next. They disappeared at Walmarts and other stores all across the country almost overnight. When people couldn't find sanitizer, they started looking for ingredients to make their own. We ran out of the ingredients. Trucks were arriving daily with fresh merchandise. Customers would time their shopping trips to arrive when the trucks were unloaded. Products would be seized up as soon as soon as associates brought it up front for stocking. Most of the sanitizers never made it to a shelf. Complaints about shortages could be heard everywhere. It was getting ugly.

On day thirty-three, I walked into work to pylons and caution tape. That morning, in every Walmart in the United States, the same thing was happening. The general merchandise and pharmacy entrance was closed and locked. The only way into any Walmart was through the grocery entrance. Orange pylons and yellow tape formed a new entrance where everyone passed to enter the store. The goal was to create an environment of social distancing to keep everyone as safe as possible form the virus. A lone Walmart customer host stood next to the exit door directing everyone through the pylons. Once inside, pylons and more yellow tape separated the entrance and exit, and customers were not allowed to cross back and forth.

Shopping at Walmart had changed overnight! Many of the approaching customers were wearing masks or facial coverings. Some were wearing gloves. There were looks of anger, confusion, and sadness. Smiles were rare. It was strange and different, and definitely not Walmart! There was a sober pall over the entire process. Nervous managers came and went, checking on security and safety.

I remember hurriedly clocking in and taking my new place outside the front door. I was stationed on the exit side, thanking customers as they left, and directing new customers to the controlled ONLY entrance to the store. Friendliness was replaced with anger and frustration. All of these directives and regulations had come from the world headquarters of Walmart. Every detail was carefully spelled out right down to how far apart each pylon was set. Careful instructions were given to associates about what to say and how customers must shop.

We found out quickly that associates were right in the middle of an impossible situation. If a customer refused to follow the new rules, management allowed them to enter the store anyway. The result was lots of anger and frustration everywhere! The rule breakers had that "Get out of the way! You can't stop me!" look as they pushed their way in, and customers coming in the right way were justifiably upset that they were being forced to shop in an unsafe environment. We were right in the middle, and everybody was upset with us. It made for a long work day! Managers were caught in between the home office and associates, and just trying to keep the store open and everyone as safe as possible. Sometimes it worked, and sometimes it didn't. Everyone, including our customers, were in unchartered waters.

Over the next days and weeks and months, changes and directives flowed from Bentonville. Fence barricades were moved and moved again. They were shortened and lengthened. Tape went up and down. It changed from yellow to orange to blue. We had one strand and then, it was changed to two. It changed back to one. The general merchandise and pharmacy entrance was reopened and closed and reopened. Hours were changed, and changed again. We went from being open 24/7 to opening at 8 to 5, then 7 to 6, and then 7 to 8, and then 7 to 10 and finally 6 to 11.

About sixty days into the pandemic, non-essential businesses were ordered closed indefinitely. People were ordered off the streets unless they were conducting essential business or working for an essential employer. School and churches were closed. Walmart was an essential business, so we were given special passes to carry with us in case police stopped us. It was bizarre!

Then the order came down that everyone shopping or working at Walmart must wear a mask covering their mouth and nose. All associates were required to enter a special entrance when coming to work. Temperatures were checked, and questions about the virus were asked each day. For a few days, some associates pushed back. There was lots of push back from the few, but in a few days about everyone was wearing a mask of some type. Walmart worked with the ones that had medical issues.

Customers were another matter. Walmart created a new morphed position, training some, and eventually all, customer hosts to be a "health ambassador". These new health ambassadors all wore black shirts, and stood at the entrance door. Looking back, those black shirts were kind of prophetic! We were living through a very dark time in civilized history. Their job was to thank those customers wearing a mask, and advise those that weren't that Walmart required all customers to wear a mask while shopping in the store. The results were mixed at best. Most of the offenders were hellbent on NOT wearing a mask under ANY conditions. We were not allowed to refuse them entrance, and management did nothing to enforce the policy. Most of the time, we caught it from both sides. The offenders were offended to be asked to wear a mask. The people wearing masks were anxious about those that didn't, or just plain angry at Walmart for failing to enforcing its own policies. We were in the middle. After a few days, most health ambassadors just stood at the door and tried to look happy, and prayed that some crazy customer wouldn't just lose it some day and hurt someone.

Our government didn't help the situation by changing positions every few days. People in the home office that had never greeted a customer entering a Walmart were driving policies that were just dumb sometimes. We never had more than about seventy-five percent of our customers wearing masks.

Sometimes it was just funny watching people showing their defiance. They wore EVERYTHING for masks. They had anything written or embroidered on them! I mean ANYTHING! There were lots of political masks. There were masks supporting all kinds of causes. There were masks calling for love and peace. There were masks with funny things on them. There were a few with crude or dirty things on them like the F-word. Hundreds of customers AND associates went around with their masks covering only their mouths. I never did get that one since the virus is primarily passed from one person to another from the nose. But nobody ever said anything. Once I saw a young man enter the store with a pair of lady's panties pulled over his head. He used the leg holes to see through. I remember praying that they were new or washed before he pulled them over his head!

In spite of everything, we got through it. Fences and barriers gradually came down. Tape was removed. Rules were relaxed. Customers could get plenty of toilet paper. Hand sanitizer could be found throughout the store, and at the end, you could buy a reusable mask for fifty cents! The world was different, and we may never get back to the way it was before the pandemic, but we survived! We had friends and family get sick, and some died. We lived through quarantines. Some of us got sick. We endured impossible situations sometimes, but we survived! The largest world retailer had a record year in spite of losing some customers forever, and we all learned a lot about ourselves and each other! It was quite a ride! I hope I never have to do it again!!!

Till Death Do Us Part

I WAS TWENTY-SIX. SHE WAS THIRTY-ONE. I WAS IN THE BANK conducting business for the company where I worked. She worked there. I was SO sick of the dating scene. She was SO beautiful. It was 1969, and I had been out of college almost four years. It seemed like every girl I dated was more interested in whether I had lettered in football, or was divorced and I was the counselor! She WAS beautiful! My question wasn't complicated, and probably most of the bank employees could answer it. She WAS beautiful! Somehow, I found my way to her desk...everyone else seemed busy. She WAS beautiful!! When she looked up and asked if I needed help, I explained why I was there. God, she WAS beautiful!! She answered my questions in a few sentences, and asked me if there was anything else. Oh my God! She was SO beautiful!!! I sputtered something about really appreciating her help, and maybe it would be fun to get together some night for a movie or dinner...she gave me her phone number! SHE GAVE ME HER PHONE NUMBER!

And that is how it began! I met the love of my life in a bank, and I knew almost from that moment that I wanted to spend the rest of my life with her! Well, not exactly, but I was definitely smitten! Shirley and I went on our first date the next week. Neither of us dated anyone else after that first date. I proposed to her three months later. She had a young daughter and was worried whether that would be a problem for me, but I assured her I didn't care. We were married June 13, 1970.

Shirley was Catholic, and I was Methodist. We attended my church together before our marriage, and I remember us discussing premarital counseling. Because of her divorce, we both wanted to get this right. My pastor didn't insist on counseling because of our age, but was willing to lead us through the process. There were three sessions. In the third session, I remember Harold telling us that every marriage union is tested. NO marriage is perfect. He talked a lot about love, and we discussed what that meant to each of us. Then, he told us something that I will never forget. He told us, "there will be a time in your marriage when one of you will want to walk away. It may be over a fight. It may be over an act of infidelity. It may be ANYTHING! But it will happen. It will test your wedding vows like never before. When that happens, one of you will have to give one hundred percent to save your marriage...not fifty percent...not sixty percent, but one hundred percent!"

Shirley and I were married thirty-nine years, seven months, and twenty-seven days. They were the best years of my life! She was the best friend I ever had! She was a business partner. She was my mentor. I loved her more than life itself...and four times, one of us had to give one hundred percent. Marriage is not perfect. It is hard work sometimes. It is a LOT about commitment.

On February 8, 2010, at 10:35 in the morning, I held my beloved Shirley as her life here on earth slowly left her. She had suffered an abdominal aneurysm. After hospital staff had exhausted all efforts to save her, they allowed us to spend her last moments on earth together.

Because of an ectopic pregnancy and issues related to that, Shirley and I never had children, but we got to watch her daughter, Sheri, grow up, marry, and have a daughter. I love Sheri like the daughter I never had.

I believe in the institution of marriage. Marriage is a contract, and it was the best deal I ever made, and I have made lots of deals! The ways people get together and stay together has always fascinated me.

Since my first day at the front door of Walmart, I am always curious what keeps people together for a lifetime. I get to meet LOTS of married couples. As I greet them, I shout out "Welcome to Walmart! We're glad you are here!" It's usually easy to spot the couples that have been married a long time. I will always walk up to them and say "How long have you been doing this together?" Then I just shut up and listen! I have heard some GREAT stories! I have seen some GREAT examples of love and devotion. The record has been seventy-three years!

I remember that couple so vividly...he early nineties, she eighty-nine. They both moved very slowly. He was in better shape than her. She needed his assistance as she walked. And what a special assistance it was! When I asked them how long they had been doing this together, he turned and literally beamed as he looked at her! "Seventy-three years! I'm ninety-one, and she is eighty-nine. We dated in high school and never dated anyone else." I remember saying, "Wow! That's a long journey! How has it been?" He just kept smiling at her, and she just kind of looked up at me and said, "Bumpy, honey, but our love always got us through it! We raised four kids, and managed to make a living. I kicked him when he got out of line!" As she said this, they looked at each other and chuckled at this private joke. I was no longer there. This trip back through memory lane was a special moment shared together while talking to a stranger in Walmart.

I spoke and broke the spell. "How did you make it happen?" I asked. "What's your secret...your advice to others?" "We've never had a disagreement that wasn't fixed before we went to bed," he volunteered. "It was hard sometimes," she said, and her gaze drifted off to some distant memories as she reflected. "God!" he said with force, and she nodded vigorously. As he said that, he reached for her hand...two bony aged hands, scarred with arthritis, squeezed together in an act of love that was so real and intense, a stranger saw the devotion that had glued this relationship, blessed by God, for so many years. I wanted to keep asking questions, but of course, I was a greeter at Walmart with a job to do, and they were a tired and aging couple that needed to get on home. I smiled and said, "Thank you for sharing with me! Thank you for the example you have been to the world for seventy-three years! Thank you for shopping at Walmart!" They both smiled and began walking to the door…holding hands…he carefully assisting the love of his life, and I returned to my work.

I remember another couple that came in two or three times a month. She did most of the shopping. He had a very alert mind but could barely walk. They always separated at the front door, and she would take her cart into the store to shop. He would get on an electric cart or wait until one is available and take off somewhere into the store. He just cruised…never bought anything, and they met up at the front door. She practically ALWAYS had to wait for him, and she practically ALWAYS carried on with me about him just goofing off and not paying any attention to time! They had been married sixty-seven years! Then, he would show up, and she would say something like, "You old reprobate! Where have you been? I was getting ready to call the police to come looking for you!" He would chuckle and reply, "Now you listen to me, woman! I'm going to have to take the switch to you when we get home!" She would laugh out loud. Then they would leave holding hands!

An update. She now comes to the store alone. When I stopped her to ask how things were going. Her smile disappeared, and she said, "Not very well." She told me her husband had just gotten too weak for her to handle. He was now in a local nursing home. It was difficult for her to talk about it, but I sensed that she was relieved to share some of her own deeply personal feelings about her world coming slowly apart. She told me every time she visited him, he started crying. She says he just cries, and says, "I want to go home."

It is difficult to know what to say at a time like that. She was heartbroken. Her situation was irreversible. There were no easy answers. The story was not going to have a happy ending. Unless….

I took her hand. I silently prayed for her and her husband. I prayed to God for the right words. It was just a very quiet moment, and I felt God's presence. I told her, "I am SO glad that God is a part of your marriage and your lives! I am SO glad that you are not in this alone! I am SO glad that God is still with your husband each time you have to leave him!" As I spoke, I felt her hands grip mine more firmly. It was as if God was just pouring strength into her tired soul! It was a Holy moment! WE were BOTH feeling God's undeniable love. At that precise time, I was just so grateful we were able to share our faiths in such a special way. I was so grateful that God let me be an instrument of His love that surpasses our human understanding!

We talked a little more about what she was doing in Walmart that day. We talked about our aches and pains. As she was getting ready to get on with her shopping, I put my arm around her shoulders, and told her, "You KNOW God's got this! Lean on Him! Lean on us! You are NEVER alone!" As she walked away, I silently said another prayer for her. She seemed to be feeling a little better, at least for a while. I had just witnessed a beautiful example of love that had been blessed by God many years ago, and was STILL as vibrant as ever! It was an example of love triumphing over impossible obstacles. It was a love that was sustaining her in the midst of her sorrow. I made a silent note to pray for all marriages that night when I got home. I would pray that they would be as good and strong as the one I had just witnessed.

A few months later. She tearfully told me her husband had died.

There are many more conversations with many more couples that I could share. They all share common denominators.

There is ALWAYS a strong sense of love in all these marriages. It is a love that has seen challenges. It is a love that has seen hardships. It is a love that has often experienced heartache. It is a love that has seen sadness. It is a love that has seen much happiness. It is a love that has endured. There is ALWAYS a willingness to forgive.

It's appropriate that I finish this chapter with the story of the second love of my life! When I was on the Kiwanis International board of directors, I met a lady from Jamaica. Andrea Scarlett was a gifted public servant and also a Kiwanian. Although we had many different perspectives, we became friends. I remember many intense online arguments about politics, but it never affected our friendship. Little did I know that she would introduce me to my present wife. It has always amazed me how God uses the most unlikely people and situations to do His work. He knew I was lonely and empty, and He used Andrea to find the most perfect partner for me... halfway around the world!

Nelia Cueno Regala lived in Mendez, Cavite in the Philippines. She was also a Kiwanian. Nelia was a widow who had managed to earn two master's degrees while raising four wonderful children and teaching school full time, all by herself. All four of her children had graduated from college. She was an active member of her Catholic church in Cavite. She also taught dancing, and led dance groups. Nelia was a friend of Andrea Scarlett, whom she had met through Kiwanis.

About three years ago, Andrea decided Nelia and I should get together, so Nelia reached out to me on Facebook. We had a lot in common, so it was a comfortable friendship. We both liked music. We cared a lot about kids. We were in Kiwanis. We shared a strong faith in Jesus Christ, and were active in our respective churches, she Catholic and me a Methodist. It was comfortable! Did I mention that she was also petite and VERY good looking?

We just seemed to connect right from the beginning. Kiwanis was a very safe subject for both of us, but that soon evolved into kids and friends and faith and everything in between. She had this great sense of humor, and I found myself looking forward to each next visit. I wasn't really looking for a relationship.

That all changed when Nelia dropped her phone and broke it. She used her phone for everything. She had never told me, but she had suffered a stroke that left her right hand too weak to write or use her computer, and she was right handed. She could text with her left hand, and that was the way she communicated online. Her money situation didn't have much wiggle room, so I told her I would send her money for a new phone. We had NEVER discussed money before, and I could tell it made her uncomfortable. I told her to think of it as a gift, not a handout, and that seemed to satisfy her misgivings. The money was sent the next day, and she was ecstatic about her new phone!

I shared the experience with a good friend a few days later, and he warned me to be careful with women from other countries. I thought this quite funny since Nelia and I had been friends for almost two years, and she had NEVER brought up money that entire time. The thought of a scam had never even entered my mind. I knew she was frugal, and lived a simple life. It was one of the things that attracted me to her. She had struggled raising her children, and sacrifice was a big part of her life.

The next time we chatted, I told her about my conversation with my friend. I was kind of making a joke about his concerns, and that was when all hell broke loose! I think her exact words were, "I don't need your damned money! I will send your money back!" That ended the conversation because she terminated the call! I had NEVER heard her swear, and she had never even gotten angry before. When I finally got her back on the phone, she was sobbing. I realized she was deeply hurt AND angry. She made it pretty clear that she had been mistaken about me.

It was like a lightning bolt! Sometimes, we just KNOW something has changed. At that EXACT moment, I KNEW I didn't want this woman to leave my life! She MATTERED to me! I wouldn't call it love, but the relationship had changed. By the way, she didn't return the money, but it took a whole lot of talking on my part to change her mind.

That whole experience led to us opening up LOTS more about our values! We talked about likes and dislikes. We talked about highs and lows in our lives. We laughed together. A few times, we cried together. She told me about each of her kids, and their incredible families. I told her about my stepdaughter, and how she seemed to be my own. We talked a LOT about our faith. The more time we spent together, the more time we seemed to WANT to spend time together! I was falling in love again although I didn't know it. Then one day, we were talking, and I told her that God seemed to be opening a door for us. She agreed that something was happening, and we began talking about how we could be together.

Love is complicated ANY time two people come together! It's REALLY complicated when those two people are half a world apart!

She spoke good English, so language wasn't a problem, but there were plenty of obstacles in our path. She had lived in the same home since birth! All four of her children had been born there. One of her sons lived a block away, and her sister lived next door to her. She would be leaving all of that. She had been a member of her church her entire life. She would be leaving that behind. Over a thirty-five-year career of teaching elementary music and art and physical education, she had made hundreds of friends. She would be leaving all of that behind. There was the matter of obtaining a US Visa and the cost of coming to the United States. Visas had gotten increasingly more difficult to obtain. The Green Card and citizenship could take up to five years and thousands of dollars. Were we prepared to make that sacrifice? Would we EVEN FEEL the same way about each other when we were finally living together? If we had a fight, it was a twenty-three-hour flight and thousands of miles before she was back home!

We decided to invite her to the United States to attend our district Kiwanis convention. If we discovered it wasn't meant to be, she would return to the Philippines. I am a past governor of the district and chair of convention resolutions. At the convention, after all the resolutions had been presented and approved, I sneaked in a final resolution with lots of 'where as' and "therefore' and finished with an announcement to the house of delegates that Nelia and I were getting married!

We were scared! We prayed a LOT! Gradually, we worked through every obstacle. As the walls kept coming down, our love kept growing! We had to WORK on our love EVERY day! Through it all, God was all over it! WE wrote our own wedding vows, and were married in my Methodist church. As Nelia recited her vows to me, she said our marriage was made in Heaven. It was! Praise be to God!!!

There were so many highs that next year. Nelia had a sparkle that just lit up a room! Her smile was golden! Everyone loved her, and I loved her more than life itself!

She loved to travel, and we visited friends in Bentonville, Arkansas. We made several trips to Branson, Missouri, and, of course, to visit my step-daughter in St. Louis.

In November 2020, we drove to Houston, Texas to visit my sister. It would be our last trip before disaster struck.

On December 4th, Nelia suffered a massive stroke that left her unable to speak, and paralyzed on her entire right side. After eighteen perilous days in Barnes Jewish Hospital in St. Louis, we brought her home.

I hired in home care for her until the money ran out, and then, took a leave of absence from Walmart. I cared for her until a septic infection took her life on November 1, 2021. Once more, I held the woman I loved while she took her final breaths.

Sometimes, life is just unfair. Nelia and I had so many plans, so many trips planned, but never taken. I give thanks to God for the time we got to share. Her legacy lives on in her four children who all call me "Dad".

I know Heaven gained two special angels when Shirley and Nelia went to their eternal home. Thank you, God...twice!

Those Carts!

Walmart has two types of carts, the types that you push, and the electric ones that are there for people with handicaps. They both generate LOTS of stories!

I spent forty-seven years in the automobile retail business. Over the years, I appraised thousands of cars and trucks. When you appraise a car, you get in it, and check out everything inside. Then, you get outside, and walk around the vehicle. You run your hand over the metal, feeling for dents or imperfections. You check for hail. You get down, and look under the vehicle. You step back, and look at the vehicle at different angles, and in different shades of light, always looking for that dent or imperfection you might have missed. You are vigilant!

That describes some people, but especially some women, when they select their cart! They will come in, usually on their phone. They will look over the carts, practically ALWAYS walking right by the carts someone just returned. All of the carts are identical except for some wear and tear. It doesn't matter!

They will pull one out from the stacked carts. They will bend over, and look at the wheels. They will still be talking on their phone, gesturing...smiling...frowning...non-stop talking. Suddenly, they will stop everything! The phone conversation is momentarily suspended. They are frowning. They bend over and look at the wheels again. The head starts moving back and forth, left and right. The appraisal is over, and the cart flunked!

The cart gets pushed aside, in the way for the next customer. The phone conversation resumes. The process is repeated. A new cart, identical to the last one, is selected and pulled out. The appraisal resumes again, look it over, check the wheels, push it back and forth. Frown! Conversation stops! Nope! This one flunked too! Now, some bad things are being said into the phone as she shares her frustration with Walmart! The second cart joins the first cart, pushed aside, and in the way for the next customer. We are rapidly making it VERY difficult for the next customer to wade through the flunked carts!

Finally, on the third attempt, she has found a cart that meets her standards...barely! She enters the store muttering about the money that Walmart makes, and expressing to her friend how SHE would fix this if she was in charge!

As she moves into the store, a man in overalls takes her place. He is joined by a retired lady talking on her phone with the speaker turned on. They both repeat the process of selecting the "right" cart. By the time they exit the cart bay, there are about ten carts pushed in a dozen directions pretty much blocking everything. Welcome to Walmart!!!

I straighten everything up, but it's a mess again soon. The really crazy thing is that the cart that wouldn't please anyone is perfect for the next customer that checks it out!

In the middle of all this chaos, a grossly overweight middle aged woman comes waddling into the store. As she comes through the second set of doors, she calls out in a loud voice, "Do you have any of them riding carts? I need one!" There are three of them charging about ten feet from where she is standing! I point them out. She hollers, "Are they charged?"

I pray to God for patience as I walk over and verify that one is ready. She hollers, "Can you bring it to me? I can't walk."

I'm praying a little harder now! My lips are probably moving. I am begging God to just get me past the next thirty-seven seconds. I unplug the cart, and drive it the twelve feet to where she is standing. She slowly gets on the cart with a lot of loud groans, and takes off into the store. There has been no "thank you" or any sign of appreciation. My prayer will continue a little longer, because I don't really know the reason for her obesity. I am not a doctor. I don't know what medical conditions she may have, and I know I have to clear my mind of all that negativity, because there are more customers entering the store behind her.

She will emerge a couple hours later with a cart full of prepared frozen foods, lots of candy and bottled sodas. There will be no fresh fruits or vegetables. We all know that good health requires physical exercise and a proper diet. Without a change in lifestyle, this woman will not live to enjoy her grandchildren. I say a silent prayer that God will open her heart and mind as she takes the cart outside to her car, and leaves it, unconcerned that SOMEONE will have to bring it in and get it charged for the next customer!

I have to ask God for another large dose of patience every few days when teenagers come in treating a cart like their personal carnival ride! The "look" is always pretty much the same. One will be pushing, and one or more will be riding. The record was four young teenage girls in one cart while one pushed, and everybody laughed. The laughs stopped when they came through the door and I lost it!

I'm pretty sure I am supposed to smile, and calmly ask everyone to get out of the cart. I may have been a little more direct that day!

Another pet peeve I have are customers who get outside with their purchases, and hop on the cart's rear frame to use it as a personal scooter as they dash across the parking lot using one leg to push while they gleefully ride to their car. One day I watched a man in his thirties or forties, and weighing over 200 pounds, take off on one of these "rides"!

And customers wonder why some of our carts "don't push very good!" It's Walmart!

Sometimes, God puts someone in my path who needs His love. When that happens, I always feel so inadequate. How can we be God's hands and feet here on earth? How can we be His instrument? How can we even know He expects us to do something? What if our actions are misunderstood? Maybe we should just let the moment pass....

I remember one of those instances. It was winter. It was cold outside, and we were having one of those rainy/snowy days when the electric carts could not go outside. Their batteries are extremely sensitive to extreme temperatures and moisture.

She approached me, and asked me if I could locate her an electric cart. She was young, probably in her early thirties, and in good health. She was obviously looking for someone else. I was lucky enough to find one at the other door, so she immediately went after it. A few minutes later, I saw her coming toward me. When she reached me. I explained about the damage that could be caused by exposing the electric carts to the bad weather, and she became very agitated. She explained to me that her husband was barely able to walk, and there was NO way he could make it into the store without her taking the cart to him.

I asked her to pull up to the entrance, and we would load him up that way. She did not like that at all, and she explained that she would probably lose her parking place while she was doing all of this, and she would make sure the cart came right back in. I explained that I understood, but if we made an exception for one, we had to let EVERYONE go outside. She angrily gave in and went out to get her husband.

A few minutes later, their vehicle pulled up in front of the entrance. I met them with the electric cart, and her husband began to exit the passenger side. I was unprepared for what I saw. He was young, probably early thirties. Every move he made was labored. She was right! He couldn't have walked the short distance into the store. He looked like he might not weigh one hundred pounds. I was overcome with emotion as I watched the scene unfold. I said a brief prayer as I stood there.

She was still irritated. It was obvious that this was not the way she wanted to handle this situation, but she immediately was by his side. She had obviously done this many times. She spoke something to him very softly, and gently assisted him onto the cart. He immediately headed inside the store, and out of the cold. She drove off to, hopefully, find their parking place again, and he patiently waited.

I returned to my duties nearer to the self-check area, and quietly reflected on what I had just witnessed. Here was a beautiful young couple in the midst of beginning their life together. They HAD to be excited about that life together and adventure that was in front of them. And then, something had happened, something life changing! Those dreams had been turned upside down. The adventure now was just getting through each day. The adventure now was just getting from the parking place to the front door of Walmart. And there he was, just quietly waiting for the woman he loved, trying to get his energy back enough to tackle another exhausting life experience.

She joined him shortly, and they headed into the store together. About an hour later, he showed up at the front door. When I approached him, he told me his wife was checking out. We began a short conversation just talking about nothing in particular. Then, I just heard this quiet voice urging me to ask him about his condition, so I asked him what was going on with his medical condition. He told me he was suffering from renal failure, totally depending on dialysis to keep him alive. He was waiting for a kidney transplant.

While he was sharing his story with me, his wife showed up. She had finished paying for their purchases, and was ready to go bring their vehicle to the door, so she could load him. I told her I would load their groceries while she helped him. She gratefully accepted.

When we were finished, she turned and thanked me for my help. She apologized for being upset earlier. The passenger door was still open, so as the two of us were standing next to her husband, I reached out and took each of their hands, and said a short prayer. I prayed for God to give each of them strength. I prayed for God to surround them with that peace and love that surpasses our human understanding. I asked God for healing. I asked the young man for his first name, and I promised to continue praying for him.

As I climbed on the cart to bring it back inside the door and park it, they pulled away. The last thing I remember was him smiling and waving.

I pray for many of our customers when I find out they are dealing with adversity. Many times, I never see them again, or I just have brief encounters as they come and go. I have to just trust that God is working in their lives.

A few months later, the young man's wife came up to me as she and their ten year-old son were leaving the store. They had been shopping, but she was very intentional in her approach to me. When she was in front of me, she reached out and took my hand. As she looked up into my face, she spoke softly. "Thank you so much for your prayers. That was such a comfort to our family. My husband didn't make it. He died twelve days ago. He just wore out."

As I tried to take it all in, and expressed my condolences, she stopped me. "No, you don't understand. After your prayer, we talked about our situation. We both knew what was in front of us. We knew that my husband might not make it. But something very special happened. Our fear of the unknown began to disappear. It was replaced with a quiet peace and acceptance. We were resolved to fight his illness any way we could, but now we were refocused on everything beautiful in our lives. We were enjoying life again! God healed him twelve days ago! He is no longer suffering. His pain is gone."

Wow! That's a lot to take in as you are standing at the door of Walmart! I was trying hard to not cry. So was she, but you could see the strength in her. Her son was looking up at both of us. I took her hand, and said a quiet prayer. "Praise be to God! Thank you for allowing this young couple to celebrate their life and many joys together. Thank you for giving them peace and understanding. Continue to surround this young woman and her son with Your love as they go forward. In the name of Jesus! Amen!"

I asked them how they were doing. She told me they were dealing with their grief. Her son smiled at me and said, " I am dealing with my grief too like my mom." I assured them that they would continue to be in my prayers. They both thanked me, and they left.

They were gone, but certainly not forgotten. They will never be forgotten! An electric cart had allowed me, once again, to see the amazing way that God works in our daily lives! An electric cart had allowed God to break through the wall of suffering and pain that a young man was experiencing, and allow him and his family to transform his final days here on earth. I was grateful to be allowed the privilege of a tiny glimpse of that transformation.

Over the years, I have been blessed with many opportunities to positively impact God's children with His love. Sometimes, they are very brief encounters, and a few sentences of encouragement. Sometimes, they are just a smile and "Good morning! We are glad you are here!" But EVERY time, I KNOW when the Holy Spirit is working! I see it in their faces! I hear it in their voices! Sometimes, it turns into something much more personal, like that young couple, but it ALWAYS happens, and a cart is the catalyst. Who would have thought that God would use a cart to touch a life!

Thank you, God, for the carts at Walmart! Thank you, God, for letting me witness your amazing power and love! Praise be to God!

Leggings and Pajamas

No book about Walmart would be complete without a few words about the crazy way some people dress, or undress, when they come shopping!

I may have to cover my eyes, or hold my nose on some of these stories, but I will do my best to help you see what I get to see every day standing at the doors of Walmart! There is really no place to start, so I will just dive in!

I have seen every type and color and print of pajamas ever made at some time or other. January and February are the worst! These people get all these pajamas at Christmas, and I guess their life is not complete until they show them off in Walmart.

The "his and hers" are the worst. One of my all-time favorites was this couple that walked into the store one afternoon. I guess they had just gotten up. They were both kind of plump; I'm being kind! They both wore matching pajamas with little candy canes, and Santa faces on them. The pajamas were white, or they had been when they were clean.

I remember he had gotten his buttons mixed up so his pajama front was crooked. He was wearing some old badly scuffed cowboy boots. His pajamas were stuffed into the top of the boots. His hair was stringy and uncombed, and he had a three day shadow. He was pretty!

She was wearing flip flops with big white fuzzy balls attached to the tops. At least, they had been white at one time. Her orange and green hair pretty much completed the picture.

He had this big lump of tobacco stuck under his tongue, bulging in his cheek. She was frantically chewing on something which must have been about twelve pieces of gum.

They must have been deeply in love or something because they were holding hands when they entered the store. Actually, they couldn't seem to keep their hands off each other!

You know you have just witnessed true love when two slightly dirty, slightly plump (I'm being kind), pajama clad people pause in the entrance of Walmart, and share a kiss with tobacco juice flowing and gum popping! Cupid must have been dancing!

If it hadn't been such a public place, I think I might have cried! Thank God I must have been busy when they left! I don't think my heart could have taken two doses of such pure affection in one day!

One day, I looked up, and this older lady was sort of hobbling into the store. She had to be well over 200 pounds, and she was wrapped in one of those fleecy bath robes with house slippers on her feet. It was cold outside, and she was not wearing a coat.

Her hair was gray with streaks of pink. Did I mention that there were a few curlers? She was headed for one of those electric carts. As she approached it, I had to look twice! She was not doing a good job of keeping the robe closed as she walked. She was wearing a shorty nightie!!!

Now, let me just say it! Women over sixty and over 200 pounds should not wear a nightie! Just when I thought I had seen everything, as she sat down, she showed me that I hadn't! All I can say is that Playboy would have been proud...or not!

I just prayed that she kept her legs together while she drove around in Walmart.

Maybe the only thing worse than some of the pajamas I have seen is the damage some women have done to leggings! For thirty-nine years, I was married to a woman who would turn over in her grave at some of the things I witness in the name of fashion.

I am a real connoisseur of sausage. Some of the best sausages are prepared and stuffed into very thin membranes. All of the sausage is contained in the membranes, and forms neatly into tightly filled links for cooking.

That process should NOT describe a woman pulling on her leggings! There need to be some basic rules about leggings. Women over 400 pounds should definitely NOT wear leggings. Women over 300 pounds should not wear leggings. Women should use mirrors when dressing in their leggings. If the body begins looking like a bulging sausage, they should choose something else. If the lady has a large rear end, (she will know), leggings are probably not for her. If she decides to wear them anyway, I am going to recommend an over garment, something that covers the sausage like area of the body. Perhaps it should extend all the way to floor, protecting the rest of the world from this unseemly sight!

NONE of these rules are followed when these women come to Walmart. The low cut ones are the worst. There just isn't enough material to go around, and they ALWAYS want an electric cart. I dread the moment when they bend over to unplug the cart.

That is ALWAYS a moment of crisis! Fabric is straining! Body parts are showing, especially posterior body parts that are best kept covered, covered really good!!!!

They don't. And the world winces, and the cart groans as they go off into the store to do their shopping! It is not a pretty sight!

I witness this sight multiple times every day. I pray for the day when leggings fall out of fashion. I am thinking that some nice tents with a little lace might make a good replacement. In the meantime, I will just pray that we don't have a riot someday when one of those leggings explodes!

Before I leave this chapter, I have to say a few words about the men. I have already addressed sagging pants in another chapter. Walmart shoppers are treated daily to a wide array of exposed men's and boy's rear ends, adorned with a wide variety of undershorts. I don't like any of it, but society does not seem to want to do anything about it, so we just continue to live and let live.

Once again, if you are over 300 pounds, you should definitely consider investing in a belt or suspenders. If you weigh over 400 pounds,

I will just pray that you are not injured when they fall. Blubber is not a good anchor!

My final pet peeve is these undershirts or sleeveless body shirts that some men wear. Walmart has a policy that you must wear a shirt when you are in the store. Some of these things barely (no pun intended) qualify.

They are the preferred attire for these guys with muscles popping out all over. They obviously lift weights, and want everybody to notice! They are easy to spot. Arms are always out and away from the body with sort of an exaggerated swinging, and fingers spread. The body is screaming, "Look at me!" I know when I see them that they are probably taking some sort of anabolic steroid or hormones. Some of these drugs can have bad effects on the human body, but these guys don't seem to care.

When I work the pharmacy door, I see them coming in all the time. They always head straight for the over the counter pharmacy products.

Perhaps some of the overweight men that I see with large pot bellies, and woman like breasts sagging toward the belt line in loose fitting body shirts SHOULD visit the pharmacy!

Better yet, maybe they should just go back home and change clothes until they lose a few hundred pounds! Guys, it's not a good look!

Walmart gets to see it all. I haven't even touched on piercings or tattoos. I haven't mentioned the shirts with all kinds of obscene words printed on them.

I have seen men and women with tattoos all over their entire bodies. I have read that excessive tattoo ink in the human body can eventually cause cancer. As we age, skin stretches and sags. I can only imagine what those tattoos will look like in a few years!

It seems to be in vogue to pierce just about every part of our bodies. I wince when some of our people come into the store. I don't understand fads that can hurt the human body. I can't imagine kissing someone with a mouth full of hardware!

Oh well! This, too, shall pass...or not. Either way, it's just another day at Walmart! I'm just trying to brace for whatever is coming next!

Donald

I can't explain it. These stories just happen! One minute I will be checking receipts, welcoming customers coming, and thanking customers going, and then it will just happen! Someone will come through that door, and you will just know that this person made a difference!

Sometimes, it takes a moment. Sometimes, it takes a few exchanges back and forth. But sometimes, you just know! It's Walmart, and I love it! I get to see God's creation in all its glory in the faces and stories tucked away in His people! That's the way it was the day I got to meet Donald!

I was busy doing whatever I do when I saw him. He was entering the grocery doors in a wheelchair. He was African American. He was being pushed by a younger lady, that I found out later, was his granddaughter.

He was thin but very alert. He was definitely a VERY senior citizen. His face was lined. He was wearing overalls and a light blue shirt. They were talking. He was smiling. And there was that cap!

VETERAN! I knew...World War II! That has only happened once before since I started working at Walmart. That story is told in another chapter in this book. There aren't many World War II veterans left. About 70 million fought in that war between 1939 and 1945, and there are approximately 119,000 veterans still alive in the United States. About 131 die every day due to old age. The men and women who fought and won that terrible war are all in their nineties or older. They were young kids! They volunteered by the millions, and endured terrible conditions around the world. They lived with terror every day. Many would die. Many more would suffer injuries that would be life changing. They were a special generation.

His granddaughter pushed him to the bench near where I stand. He gingerly climbed out of the wheelchair, and took his seat. I walked over and spoke to him, and began a conversation that would change that day for me forever!

I introduced myself, and he told me his name was Donald. I thanked him for his service, and asked him if he was a World War II veteran. He confirmed what I already knew. I asked him how old he was, and he told me he was ninety-seven. He told me it was hard for him to walk long distances, but he assured me that he was more than able to walk and care for himself. He was living with his granddaughter, and had spent his entire life in the small town of Charleston, Missouri. Charleston is just fifteen miles from Sikeston in the fertile boot heel of Southeast Missouri.

As I thanked him and held his hand, he looked at me and smiled. His smile was from the heart. It instantly cut through all the craziness and busyness of that day! I was quietly thanking God for putting this special man in my path!

I looked at him, and asked, " Can you tell me a little bit about when and where you served?" He quietly began telling his story.

"I was just sixteen. Me and two friends lied about our age and volunteered. Lots of kids were doing that, and they didn't seem to care too much. They needed soldiers. We joined the army. We were sent to the Philippines."

It suddenly hit me. It was 1942. He was black. The military was still segregated back then. So I asked him, "How was it being black in a white army?" He looked down at the floor, and then looked back up to me, straight into my eyes. With a sad smile, he told how hard it was. "We were scared every day. I spent three years there, and we cried ourselves to sleep nearly every night. We had to stay off base because black men were not allowed to live in the same barracks as white men."

"They didn't allow us to have weapons, so we would sneak onto the base at night and steal rifles and ammunition. They knew but they just looked the other way. The next day we would fight the enemy side by side with white soldiers. That night, we would return to our separate quarters, sneak back on base, and steal more bullets to fight another day."

As he talked, there was no anger or bitterness in his voice. There was just a quiet gentle sadness as he told this amazing story about a young black man, halfway around the world, fighting in a frightening, bloody, deadly war, separated from his white brothers during the night, and fighting beside them every day. His voice was strong. He was remembering, and I could see it etched in every line in his face. I could see it in those sad eyes, shaded by that dark blue cap with "Veteran" inscribed above its bill. He was remembering.

It was a powerful moment. He was reflecting on the sacrifice and the blood that was shed for our freedom, and I was reflecting on a young kid that should have been back home in school doing whatever young kids do when they are sixteen. But back then, many segregated schools only had eight grades. I was reflecting on a young scared black kid fighting for his country in an army that did not yet accept him because of his color.

I asked him why he did it, and his words will stay with me forever! " I did it because I live in the greatest country on earth! I did it because I love my country! I did it to protect us back home! God bless America!"

I took his hand, and shook it. I was overcome with emotion and gratitude for this old man who had selflessly and courageously fought for my freedom so many years ago. I thanked him again for serving his country, and returned to my duties at the front door.

People were coming and going, but I was still caught up in what I had just heard and witnessed. A young woman was entering with her three children. Two of the children looked like they might be in the third or fourth grade. The youngest looked like she might be in preschool or kindergarten.

I approached and greeted them, and asked them if they could spare a few minutes to touch the life of a stranger. The mother looked a little uncertain, so I quickly told them the story I had just witnessed. As I spoke, I could see the uncertainty in the mother's face melting away. She bent over, and whispered something to her children, and then they headed over to where Donald was sitting.

As they approached, he looked up. I could tell he didn't understand yet what was about to happen. The two little girls and little boy stopped about three feet from him. They were nervous, and a little awkward, but that innocent sweetness, that only our very young all have, took over.

The oldest little girl shyly thanked him for his service. The little boy was next. Finally, the youngest little girl stepped forward. She was braver than her older brother and sister,, and she proudly thanked him as she dazzled him with her smile.

Mother just quietly looked on as she watched her children learn a life lesson about our country and those that have protected it. When they finished, and she stepped forward, he stood up, and everyone knew he was having a very special day. There were hugs and lots of smiles all around. He sat back down, and they started to return to their shopping.

Suddenly, they all stopped again, and I could see mom having an animated conversation with her children. They returned, and the mother asked if she could take her children's picture with him.

He stood. The children surrounded him. The two oldest grasped his hands. The little girl wrapped her hands around his leg. All shyness was gone, replaced with a newfound love and pride. As mom snapped her pictures, special smiles lit up Walmart! A proud veteran knew once again that his sacrifice had mattered, and a young mother and her children had gotten a history lesson and an affirmation of love that would stay with them for the rest of their lives...and I got to see it all!

Special Needs and Disabilities

I remember a Kiwanis International convention in Montreal, Canada, a few years ago. A dance troupe, dressed as Disney characters, came out on stage and performed an incredible dance routine to the music, "It's a Small Small World." The synchronization and acrobatic stunts were performed to perfection. After the program was over, each of the dancers removed their head sets and were introduced individually. Every performer had some sort of disability or special need. Some had difficulty expressing themselves, but they had come together as one, and put on a performance that would challenge ANYONE! The audience went crazy! The applause was thunderous!

These young people were all members of a Kiwanis sponsored Aktion Club from central Canada. Their club sponsor was a professional dance instructor.

More than 11,000 adults with disabilities around the world are involved in this Kiwanis-family program, developing leadership skills while working with others to help those in need. These Aktion Clubs empower members to be themselves, work together with friends, and implement plans through action.

It is a great example of how every life matters!

Fifteen per cent of the world's population have some sort of disability according to UNICEF. That is at least one billion people. About 240 million of them are children.

These people live in every community. They deal with all kinds of barriers that limits their ability to function in daily life.

Some of these barriers are buildings, or doors, or toilets, or playgrounds. Some of these barriers are communication issues such as text books unavailable in braille.

One of the biggest challenges the disabled face is the attitudes of the general public. Stereotyping, low expectations, pity, condescension, harassment or bullying can make their lives more difficult.

I am proud and grateful that I work for a company that does none of these things! Every part of the Walmart Superstore where I work addresses people with disabilities. You can expect the same policies in every Walmart! There are ramps at the entrances and all exits. Entrance doors automatically open and close. Toilets are specially equipped. Faucets have sensors that do not require them to be manually turned on and off. People with sight issues can request an associate to assist with their shopping. That service is actually available to anyone that requests it.

Working with and serving people with disabilities is an important and ongoing part of Walmart training. Many people with disabilities work or shop at Walmart, and the company takes its responsibilities very seriously. Associates who violate these policies are coached.

During my entire time with the Sikeston Walmart Superstore, I have had the honor and privilege to work alongside John! EVERYONE loves John! He works in maintenance and assists with janitorial duties. From time to time, he also has worked outside, helping to push shopping carts. He has been a part time associate for over nine years.

John loves cowboy boots, and has several pair. They are always polished to a high gloss! When he is off the clock, he can always be seen walking at a very fast clip up and down the aisles, adorned with his cowboy hat, big shiny belt buckle, and those cowboy boots.

The smile is broad, and lights up the store! The cell phone is tightly clutched, and held out in front of him as he walks. The look is intense. You can hear music coming from the phone as he approaches.

And John is singing! John is singing! John LOVES to sing! He knows the words to hundreds of songs! He is walking with great big long strolls and singing.

The voice will never win an award, but the music coming from his soul warms hearts throughout the store! Customers will pause and smile. Some customers have become his best friends! There will be quick "high five" hand slaps! Sometimes, there will be a warm hug!

The spontaneous joy pouring from this young man is contagious! John is making a difference!

When this young man's break is over, he will return to his work. In one of those perplexing puzzles of life, this special young man who has hundreds of songs committed to memory, will quietly tell you, as you give him work instructions, to have him do just one or two duties at a time, so he won't get confused or mixed up.

As he tells you this, the sincerity and desire to please is always there. John makes a difference!

Away from the store, John lives with a roommate. He told me someone comes in and assists with cooking and household chores. When I asked him how he liked to spend his spare time, he mentioned mowing grass.

Then, he surprised me, and told me he enjoyed preaching! That was a curve ball! I didn't see that coming!

When I asked him where he preached, you could hear the quiet pride in his voice as he told me, "I read my Bible, and preach in the kitchen!"

I have never seen John preach, but I have seen him sing many times. In my mind, I can envision him with his bible in his hand. I can see him walking back and forth in that kitchen proudly sharing God's word! The nervous energy will be poured into the sermon! The congregation may be small, but I guarantee you Jesus is watching, and hanging on every word! He is looking down from Heaven, and smiling at His faithful servant!

John is doing what John does best, making the world a better place!

Samuel is a recent part-time addition to our asset protection team. Samuel has no arms below the elbow. He has no legs. He walks with the aid of artificial prosthetics. When I approached him about sharing his story, he was excited to share his amazing life!

Samuel was born in Vietnam. He never knew his real parents, and lived in a Vietnamese orphanage until he was four.

He was adapted by an American family who traveled all the way to Vietnam to get him. Sam grew up in Sikeston, Missouri, with five siblings, all of whom were adapted and also had some sort of disability.

After watching this amazing young man do his job for a few days, I wanted to share his story with the world! I have visited with him several times about wanting to include him in this book. He has lived through so many challenges in his short life (he just celebrated his nineteenth birthday) that I was uncomfortable with sharing some of the deeply personal things he cheerfully shared with me.

In his quiet way, he assured me it was okay. In addition to not having arms or legs, he has had to deal with dyslexia, speech impairment, learning challenges, and word processing.

As he talked about all of these things, I couldn't help but think of my precious Nelia in the aftermath of her stroke. Samuel told me that he has been told by doctors that he may have had some brain damage at birth.

In spite of all of these challenges, this young man practices martial arts, lifts weights at the local YMCA, drives himself, shaves, and feeds himself! He graduated from our local high school!

When I complemented him on all of his achievements, he smiled, and said, "I'm lousy with math, and I'm not good at financial management."

He candidly admitted that he did not relate well to kids. He attributes all of this to the brain damage he suffered as a baby. He had to deal with bullying in school, and fought depression in his early teens.

When I asked him how he got through it all, he flashed that big smile and told me he was "The New Sam!" He gives ALL the credit to God! Everything changes about Sam when he talks about Jesus! He becomes animated! His voice takes on a new kind of intensity! He is a GREAT disciple! The world needs more Sam's!!! His story is a great example of how we can overcome huge obstacles in our path through faith and determination! Go, Sam!!!

Thank you, Walmart, for making stories like Sam and John possible, and your commitment to hire the handicapped and people with special needs. That commitment is not only changing their lives, but is changing our lives that get to work beside them!

I have gotten to meet MANY people, young and old, with disabilities. Some of them are able to do things by themselves, and some have caregivers. They are ALL special!

There are two young women that I see almost every week. One always comes into the store in a wheel chair, pushed by a family member. Her legs are disproportionately smaller than her upper body. I don't think she can walk.

I don't know the cause of her disability, but I DO know the power of her smile! As we have sort of gotten to know each other, we have this routine.

When I see her, I throw out my arms, outstretched in greeting! I will always exclaim, "Wow! Look who's back! Welcome to Walmart! You have just made my day better...AGAIN!!!"

This will always bring a broad and engaging smile from her and her family. She will usually say something back, and they will go on into the store. I hope, each time, that she somehow knows that she just made a difference! I KNOW she just made MY life better witnessing that beautiful spirit on full display to the world!

The second young lady always rides in a shopping cart. Her legs are much smaller than her upper torso. She is very small, and I have never seen her speak, but she always smiles when I welcome her.

I am reminded, over and over, that smiles speak a universal language.

Every day, I see several stroke victims. A few must have a wheel chair, or use an electric cart. Most walk, some better than others. Strokes are devastating! I watched my precious Nelia go from a vivacious, energetic, graceful, and beautiful woman to a drawn up and withered little soul who could no longer walk or talk, paralyzed on one side, and confused about simple tasks.

I know the walk. I recognize the drawn up hand. I always make a special effort to give these people EXTRA encouragement. They get a more special welcome. I make a point to complement them in their battle against the challenges they now face.

Universally, I am always rewarded with a smile, some more crooked than others, but always a smile that says, "I will overcome!" The raw courage of some of these men and women who have had their lives snatched from them is amazing!

I have shared the story of Wanda in another chapter, but I have seen so many stroke stories walk into Walmart!

There is Jim, who usually comes in on Thursdays. He is always pushing his shopping cart with his walker in the cart. He walks very slowly. He limps badly, and sort of drags one leg. He gets tired, and has to stop and rest frequently, but he turns down offers for help.

His wife is an invalid, and he is her caregiver. He was a tax accountant before his stroke, and he is no longer able to work full time, and he has lost some of his skills. We have a short visit every week. His inner strength and faith always show through.

When he leaves, his cart is piled high and overflowing. The trip has taken him two to three hours, and he is always exhausted, but he gives me a thumbs up with his good hand, and a big smile. I know the struggle hiding behind that smile, and that smile is always one of my best treats that day.

Whenever I see him coming, I pause for a moment to say a quick prayer to God to give him strength, and to surround him and his wife with that love and peace that surpasses our human understanding. Jim is a hero that will not be defeated!

I haven't seen Jim for a few weeks. I don't know why, but God knows! I pray for Jim and his wife wherever they go.

There are so many among us like the people in these stories! Every one of them has a story! Every one of them need our prayers, and our encouragement, and our support! Every one of them is special. We can learn so much from them about dealing with the adversities in life! They truly make a difference!

If one of you are one of these people, I give thanks for your life, and the difference you make! You make us stronger when we see YOUR will to overcome!

Store Number 9

By 1968, Sam Walton had opened eight stores. His first store was in Rogers, Arkansas, founded in 1962, but by 1968, Sam Walton was feeling restless. Sales in his company had reached $12.6 million in 1967, and his vision was reaching beyond Arkansas.

His search would take him to Sikeston, Missouri. I have spent a lot of time wondering why he would choose Sikeston as his first location in the state of Missouri. He was an engaging and smart entrepreneur. Maybe he had read the article in the *St. Louis Globe Democrat* in April 20, 1947, mentioning that Sikeston, Missouri was rumored to have more millionaires per capita than any other city in the United States. That would have certainly interested him. Maybe he had driven through the area and observed some of the most fertile, high producing farm land in the world.

Sam Walton attended the opening of his new store. He would not have guessed that, in 1968, at the opening of the store in the Sikeston Midtowner Village shopping center, that he would become one of the richest men in America in an extraordinary career of merchandising and development. That store would become known in Walmart as "Store Number 9". There are now over 10,000 Walmart stores operating in twenty-four countries under forty-six different names.

By the time I was hired in October 2016, the store was in its third Sikeston location, having outgrown each of the two previous locations. It had found its new home on South Main Street in a sprawling 230,000 square feet building. A typical Walmart has about 120,000 items of various categories for sale.

Bananas are Walmart's top selling product, about 1.5 billion pounds every year. There are about 330 million rolls of toilet paper sold in Walmart stores every week. Groceries make up about fifty-six percent of total sales; no wonder Walmart began opening super stores in the early 2000s.

By my calculations, I am estimating the annual sales tax paid to Missouri, the local county, and Sikeston from Store Number 9 will be about $10,800,000 this year. The payroll to 300 to 350 associates will turn about seven times in the local economy, adding another annual impact of between 80 and 90 million dollars. Walmart makes a difference! Store Number 9 makes a difference!

Over the years, I have heard lots of criticism of Walmart destroying American businesses when they come to town. I strongly disagree!

Competition has been the corner stone of the American economy forever. As a manager and then owner of General Motors dealerships, I remember having constantly to adjust, and readjust to the competition. We overcame the odds by doing what we were good at, and outworking the competition.

Sam Walton understood that business principle. You look at the business model you have carved out for yourself. You look at the market you are serving. You look at your competition, and you go to work. You try to work harder and smarter. He did both!

Sam Walton's business model was to sell things for less. He accomplished this by logistics, making sure that his stores were within a day's drive from the warehouses that serviced the company. This, and his buying strategy, allowed him to sell name brand products at a lower price than his competition.

Sixty years later, the company still applies this simple philosophy. Nobody has been able to copy Walmart and do a better job. As online sales carve a bigger percentage of retail sales every year, no company is better poised than Walmart to meet this challenge. The 10,000-plus large super stores can easily be converted to distribution centers. Walmart associates can easily be retrained from retail to an online business model.

I have a lot of respect for Walmart. Not only have they treated me with respect and fairness, they worked with me with compassion when I had to have surgeries, and especially when my precious Nelia had her stroke. When the money ran out, they allowed me to take an extended leave of absence as her caregiver.

I live in Sikeston. I have spent my entire seven-and-a-half years at Store Number 9. I absolutely love the Walmart story! I hope I am not violating company policy by expressing my personal feelings about things I wish were different, but since it's my book (smile), I will mention a few things that I think would make the company better. I hope they listen. I feel compelled to write this chapter even though it may be more interesting to associates than our customers.

Most of this book has dealt with the people that come and go every day through our doors. But associates come and go every day as well. This chapter will talk about the people that make Walmart possible. This chapter will talk about the associates that Sam Walton loved! This chapter is a chapter that may be more interesting to the 1.5 million people working for Walmart in the United States than to others reading this book. Anyway, here goes!

Employee turnover is a difficult expense to estimate, and Walmart has lots of turnover. That is not all Walmart's fault. Today's work ethics in the marketplace play a significant role. Nevertheless, even though it is not a line item on an expense analysis, it increases expenses, and it hurts productivity.

As a "good will" ambassador standing every day at the front door, I talk to many of these associates. Over my years in management and ownership, I have learned two things about employees.

The lazy and work dodgers never stop being lazy and work dodgers. If they are not made to improve, they poison a good work force.

Good workers never stop being good, even when they are frustrated or are not recognized for their achievements. If their own company does not see this, and act on it, the competition sees it, and draws them away. The number of new Walmart associates that make it to five years is too low.

The comments I hear from these associates on their way out the door, and when they come back to shop after quitting is always the same. "I am now making three, four, five, six dollars more." "I just got tired of doing all the work when lazy people were always calling in or not made to do their jobs, and the rest of us had to do it all!" "Nobody appreciated me." "I just couldn't support my family."

When I was drowning in phone calls and complaints in my dealership, the turning point was empowering my management. Then, we empowered everyone. EVERYONE had a stake, and they were rewarded.

I didn't have to expose or track down the lazy employees that didn't care. My employees did it for me. These people were called in. Problem employees were dealt with. If there was not noticeable improvement, they were terminated.

I hope Walmart takes a hard look at empowering associates who have been with the company over five years. Granting them more limited authority would improve company morale, improve customer satisfaction by providing faster service and assistance, and take pressure off of coaches and team leads trying to cover 230,000 square feet of geography. I am glad they are considering bringing back bonuses based on profitability and performance.

Walmart is not only good at selling things, they are apparently good at match making as well! A couple came in the other day, and shared that they had been married forty-three years. They had both worked at the original Sikeston Walmart while they were high school students.

Walmart used to have "Blue Light Specials." They had met under the Blue Light Special, and Cupid must have been close by. They began dating, and the rest is history. Unfortunately, I got busy, and we did not get to finish our conversation. I hope I get to hear the rest of the story someday. They did share that they both got to meet Sam Walton.

When I shared their story in the break room, Ginger remembered the Blue Light Specials. She has worked for Walmart for thirty-eight years. Ginger is one of my favorite employees. She is a loyal and hard worker, and she is always eager to help others, whether it is a customer or an associate.

Apparently, Cupid did not pack his bags after bumping into that young couple. He still seems to be flying around Walmart. Walmart does not prevent associates from dating as long as it does not affect their job and there is no work conflict of interest. I have seen a number of romances blossom at Store Number 9.

One of my favorites is Greg and Vicki. They work in different departments, but it is always a joy when they get to share a break together. They can be seen holding hands as they head outside. A few minutes later, they can be seen returning to work, and sharing their lives together. God is good!

Another Vicki and I go to church together. We sing in the choir together. We have even performed duets together. Vicki has worked for Walmart for thirty-four years. She is one of our most senior cashiers.

Teresa, Ginger, and Rachelle have all worked for Walmart for over thirty-five years. There are dozens of associates who have become my friends. Tammy, who works with me as a customer host, can be a hoot, and she has this deeply spiritual side that endears her to our customers.

In many ways, a lot of us are like an extended family. We deal with the same public challenges every day. We work long hours, and share many of the holidays. Walmart only closes two days a year, Christmas and Thanksgiving, and Thanksgiving has just been added since COVID. We spend time together in the break room.

And sometimes, we grieve together. I remember Betty and Lulu. I talk about them in another chapter. When Walmart associates go on to their eternal reward, we mourn.

Then, there was this young man who started out as a cart pusher, and then transferred to the front door as a greeter/customer host during COVID. Hunter had graduated with honors from high school, and was enrolled in college pursuing a degree in Education. His dream was to be a high school history teacher.

Hunter took me into his confidence on just about everything. We talked about girls. I helped him through his depression after he and his high school sweetheart broke their engagement. We argued over fraternities. There were discussions about God and faith. There wasn't much that was off limits.

After he quit his job at Walmart, we still talked on the phone from time to time. Now and then, I would get a text. He was very popular in his fraternity. We argued sometimes when he partied too much, but his grades never suffered. He was on the Dean's Honor Roll every semester. You just knew this young man was going to go on to make a difference.

I remember him coming to our local high school to do his student teaching. The kids loved him, and his teacher mentor, who is a personal friend of mine, praised him. Hunter nailed it like he seemed to nail everything!

We talked. The final year of college would be starting in a few weeks. He had just made the spring dean's honor list again! Life seemed perfect...but it wasn't. Hunter took his life in his college fraternity house on August 16, 2023.

The world stopped for some of us that day that knew him. My prayer for Hunter was that he finally found the peace that alluded him in life. It is still hard to not feel guilty for failing to be that anchor he apparently was so desperately seeking while keeping those demons a secret from all that knew him.

I remember going through some very dark times a few years ago when suicide became an option that I wrestled with every day. My friends and family, the journal that became this book, and my faith got me out of that abyss. Mental illness and depression are enemies of the soul!

Hunter, you are missed! You mattered! You made a difference! Peace be with you, my gentle young friend!

There are so many associates who have become my friends during this journey. I have seen them come and go, but we form a special bond. Working with the public can be stressful and tedious sometimes.

Working with the public at Walmart can take you to places you have never been! We lift each other up, and we become one.

Somehow, Walmart makes it all work. It's not always pretty, but it's impressive! Worldwide sales in the year ending in January 2024 were 642 billion dollars! Store Number 9 was a part of that!

The delicate balance between the public and associates and management is a tight rope walk sometimes. Black and white issues are usually pretty easy to navigate. It is the gray issues that drive me crazy!

"The customer is always right." overrides common sense and fairness sometimes. When there is a conflict, management will usually take the customer's side. This is frustrating to me, and, over the past seven-and-a-half years, it is one of the biggest frustrations from my fellow and sister associates.

I will give an example. We have a sign on the door that has been there for the entire time I have worked at Walmart. It states that service dogs are welcome, and pets are not allowed. The law clearly states that service animals must be under control.

We get lots of training about our boundaries in these situations. If a customer enters the store with an animal, we are allowed to ask if it is a service dog, and explain that pets are not allowed. If the customer states the animal is a service animal, we are to allow them entry.

One day, two women entered the store pushing a shopping cart with a small dog in the cart. There was nothing in the cart between the dog and the cart, which is required by state food laws. The dog had no collar, and no leash.

I stopped them, and explained the Walmart policy regarding service animals and pets as displayed on the entrance doors. Both ladies started swearing, and one of them told me the dog was a service animal, and it was none of my f...ing business. I kept my cool, and told them the dog was not on a leash, and had no collar, and that animals had to have tags with proof of their shots and under control on a leash.

The women went ballistic and demanded to see a manager. I politely told them they could go to the service desk, and ask for a manager. Walmart's service animal policy was clearly on display, and I had accurately stated it. I knew I was on solid ground regarding dog collars and leashes. Besides, the front end coach had just reminded me the day before that we needed to toughen up on allowing pets in the store. He had assured me that I would be backed when customers objected.

A few minutes later, I saw the women headed into the grocery area with one of them carrying the dog. It was no longer in the shopping cart, but there was clearly no collar or leash. A little later, the coach came and told me I was wrong about the law. Leashes and collars are not required in public places! I could not prevent them from entering the store.

It got worse. When the women finished their shopping, and were leaving, I got the middle finger, and a string of cuss words, ending in the familiar, "F-you!"

When these kinds of things happen that shouldn't happen, it's hard for associates to put on our "happy" face.

Management might disagree with me, but in my mind, our other customers had to put up with another pet in the store, or a service animal that was not properly or safely collared and leashed. An associate had to "suck it up" for the next customer, and a very rude pair of ladies was allowed to be their bully selves with no accountability.

I DID suck it up, and I WAS ready for the next customer, but it took a few minutes in a corner and a very intense prayer to get my collective self under control. Thank you, Jesus!!!

A few years earlier, if that situation had occurred in my dealership, I would have walked to the front door, and when the situation was explained, I would have asked the customers to leave, and return with the dog properly collared and leashed. I would have supported my employee who was clearly right, and a potentially bad situation would have been over before it started.

Bad customers are not needed, and should not be welcome in ANY business! The F-word should not be tolerated! The F-word should be grounds for ANY customer to be ordered out of the store IMMEDIATELY!!! I hear customers using it every day!

Over the past seven years, I have worked under two store managers, close to twenty coaches (formerly assistant managers), and more than twenty team leads formerly customer service managers). Coaches get transferred from store to store as part of their ongoing training, so our eight to ten coaches have changed from time to time.

Hourly associates work most closely with team leads. These are some of the most amazing people in the entire Walmart management chain! The company would have difficulty achieving its goals without them. Sometimes, I think they are some of the least appreciated and rewarded. That is unfortunate.

When I talked to some of the team leads in Store Number 9, they all expressed that one of the things they liked best about their jobs was getting work in the whole store, and connecting with people, both customers and associates.

While people were one of the things most team leads liked about their jobs, people were also one of their greatest frustrations. Another frustration was a lack of consistency from upper management, and nobody liked the changes in shifts. Most Walmart stores are open from 6 a.m. to 11 p.m. Walmart does this crazy thing where they have associates work from 2 p.m. to 11 p.m., and then open the next morning at 6 a.m. to 3 p.m. I have heard the same complaints from coaches.

That is brutal on the human body! The body needs rests, and it does not usually adjust quickly to these shift changes. Compare it to flying from one country to another. When it is time to go to bed, the body is still wide awake. When it is time to get up, the body is still asleep.

I personally think that a day off in between these swing shifts should be mandatory, or they need to be done away with all together. Oh well!

That aside, most of these team leads are remarkable in their jobs, but they are all overworked. Burnout occurs frequently. Too many of them leave the company, or return to their previous job as an hourly associate. This comes with a cut in pay which is preferred to the punishing schedule they had as a team leader. This is always sad to me because these are some of the best people in all of Walmart. I only have Store Number 9 as a reference, but I suspect this issue is the same throughout the company

Walmart has a really good plan here with their team leads, but I hope they figure this out. It costs thousands of dollars to develop an employee, and everything is affected when it doesn't work out.

Store Number 9, you have impacted thousands of associates since 1968. You have seen millions of customers come through your doors. You have been a major contributor to the economies of several counties and cities in Southeast Missouri for over half a century! Thank you, Store Number 9! Thank you, Sam Walton, for believing in Sikeston, Missouri, and so many more communities around the world!

Let Freedom Ring

As I try to bring this book to a close, no cause is greater to me than the cause for freedom! It has defined my life from my birth to this moment in the fourth quarter of my time here on planet earth.

I was born to a mother and father who were born in the early 1900s before the Depression. My father told stories of using horses and mules to plow the family farm. My mother talked about riding in a horse-drawn wagon to make trips to town. They grew up in western Kansas, and got married just in time to begin their lives together during The Great Depression.

Life was so hard that they migrated to the west coast, and settled in Oregon where logging the bountiful forests was booming. My father was badly injured when a log rolled over him and broke over one hundred bones in his body. After spending over a year in the hospital and enduring dozens of surgeries, he limped out of the hospital, loaded his family and all their possessions in their old car, and returned to their roots in Kansas.

With every penny they had saved, and a LARGE loan from the local bank, my parents purchased 640 acres in southwest Kearny County, Kansas. That farm would support them for the next thirty years while they raised their four children. Pat, Leroy (Buddy), and I would grow to adulthood, and live successful and fruitful lives. Larry would die while serving in the Vietnam conflict.

They would sell the farm's surface rights in 1971, but keep the bountiful mineral rights buried beneath the dry soil. Those mineral rights included a share of the Hugoton Gas Field, which covered parts of Kansas, Oklahoma, and Texas. Gas royalty checks from producing natural gas wells on the farm would support them the rest of their lives. A thirty-six-inch pipeline, to transport the gas across the United States, crossed the family farm.

After the pipeline was laid, wildcatters began drilling wells all over the three states, and large companies were formed to buy up these wells and provide energy for the entire country and other parts of the world.

Those wildcatters were incredible people. They were engaged in a business that was anything but a sure thing. But the Hugoton Gas Field was so big and so rich that many of them became very wealthy. Entrepreneurs formed companies. Companies would become big companies. Big companies would buy other big companies. Big companies would become giants in the gas and oil industry.

Over the years, the companies owning the rights to those minerals under our farm have changed many times, but the monthly royalty checks have come every month for over sixty years.

This story could only happen in America. I got to grow up in the American dream! Let freedom ring!

Our forefathers understood this. They had lived through tyranny and excessive taxes levied by the British Crown. They saw the dangers of overzealous government bringing down oppressive controls over its citizenry. This would culminate in the Revolutionary War as the colonies fought for their independence from England.

At the war's successful conclusion, those thirteen colonies would come together in Philadelphia, and draft the Declaration of Independence in 1776. The Constitution would follow in 1787. The Bill of Rights was proposed to the congress in 1789. These three documents still govern our country 248 years later with only twenty-seven amendments. No other country in the history of the world has ever duplicated or exceeded the accomplishments of this great country. Let freedom ring!

Our freedoms are the cornerstones to these three great documents that provided the foundation for our country. The only stain on this great story was the allowing of slavery which was finally abolished in 1865.

The Walmart story could not have been written in any other country. Walmart was founded in 1962 in Rogers, Arkansas by brothers Sam and James "Bud" Walton, and incorporated under Delaware General Corporation Law on October 31, 1969. After just five years of rapid growth, Sam Walton opened the first store outside of Arkansas in Sikeston, Missouri, the store where I work, and where all of the stories in this book, but one, have occurred. The Sikeston store was Number 9. I have written a whole chapter about Store Number 9.

Today, Walmart has over 10,000 stores worldwide, operating in twenty-seven countries, and employing 2.1 million people. Let freedom ring!

Its net revenue exceeded $605 billion in 2023. Walmart owned Sam's Club centers produced another $84 billion. Seventy-one percent of the United States population used Walmart. Ninety-six percent know Walmart. Let freedom ring!

The company spent #3.41 billion in advertising in 2022. I could not find information on 2023. Seventy-five million products are listed on Walmart.com. 407.8 million people visited Walmart in one month in 2022. Let freedom ring!

A few months ago, a service repairman was working on the automatic doors at the grocery entrance in the Sikeston Walmart where I work. The doors are the original doors, installed when the super center opened in the early 2000s. There apparently is some sort of counter on the doors that keeps track of the times they open and close. After some checking, he told me they had opened and closed over 22 million times! Sikeston has a population of 16,291 as of 2020. That means a number equal to Sikeston's population came and went through the Sikeston Walmart's doors 141,182 times since it has opened! Let freedom ring!

The story of America has filled many books. I only include a few small pieces of my country's amazing story because it has impacted my OWN story from birth! I have been blessed with so much as a citizen of this great country! Let freedom ring!

But freedom and liberty are fragile. They were fragile when our founding fathers were drafting the documents that still guide us as a country today. They have been attacked by misdirected zealots throughout history.

Those attacks have never been greater than today. Our country is deeply divided between two political parties that have radical differences on how to lead our nation. Sitting between these two chasms is a group of independent thinkers that are all over the political spectrum.

The future of the United States of America will hinge on how well those wildly diverse factions can find common ground and move forward. Our enemies and allies wait and watch on the sidelines to see how this story will play out.

I see the division and anxiety every day as thousands come through the doors of one of America's greatest success stories! I struggle with my own emotions and values like many of my friends. I couldn't even write this book in many countries of the world. In others, I would have to seek government's oversight before I could go forward.

So my plea to all who read this book is for you to examine YOUR own life, and how it has been shaped by the country we all call our home. Ask yourself how it would be different if you had been born and lived in another country. Take a little time and read or re-read the Declaration of Independence. Take a hard look at the Constitution. Pay particular attention to how these documents all talk about your basic rights and privileges as a citizen of the United States.

Now, remove those rights and privileges from those three documents, and reexamine how your life might be different. That is a process that I have tried to apply in my own discernment, and it changes my perspective dramatically.

I take solace that our forefathers fought and wrestled with these same questions. Sometimes, it was not pretty. The good news is that they did not give up, and the end result was three documents that have been the foundation of this great nation for almost 250 years! Let freedom ring!

God has helped me a lot as I have tried to stay the course. I will be talking more about that in the final chapter of this book.

Recently, I have added some new disciplines to my life to help me be a better citizen. I visit cemeteries frequently, and look for tombstones of young soldiers. The dates help me find the ones who died, fighting for my liberty. I always say a prayer for them and their families. It is a sobering and powerful experience to share those moments with someone who paid the ultimate price for you and me to protect our freedoms and way of life.

I spend more time in public places and parks just staring at our flag, and reflecting the storied history of our country.

I have coffee regularly with a good friend, and the conversations always get around to freedom.

It was appropriate that I spent a little time in this book to talk about my country and the freedoms I enjoy. In the seven years I have spent writing this book, I have seen just about everything coming through the doors of Walmart. I have been hugged, kissed (once), cursed, shoved, tripped, and knocked down (once). It's been fun, sad, comical, maddening, enlightening, and inspirational. It has NEVER been boring.

I have seen the best and worst of my country, and everything in between, and I wouldn't live anywhere else!

I've watched thousands of kids and young people come and go. Some needed a good spanking, but most were quite a bit like I was at their age. They were full of life! They were full of energy! Sometimes, it spilled over. Most of their values mirrored my values, even if they expressed them in different ways. They ALL had cell phones! If there was one thing I could change in their lives, it would be to just put those phones away, and look around them at this beautiful diverse place we call the Unite States of America. I believe most of them will figure it out just like we did.

Freedom is a gift from God, and paid for by the blood of many. We are the greatest country in the world. The stakes are high! I hope that those that read these words take their own journey, reflecting on this country, and what it means to them. I pray that we get it right!

God bless America!

Let freedom ring!

God and Me

God has walked beside me through every page in this book. It's only appropriate that I talk a little bit about that relationship in this final chapter.

I have always been grateful for growing up in a Christian home. I cannot manage a life without God as my partner. That relationship has grown exponentially since 2010 when I lost my first wife. Depression became a daily battle after she died. To say I struggled would be an understatement.

After spending my entire adult life being an encourager and motivator to others, I suddenly found myself avoiding people. I moved to the back row of church on Sunday mornings, and left before the service ended. I caught myself breaking down and crying for no reason.

When I talked to my family doctor, who was also a friend from church, he suggested that I consider writing a journal. That began a ritual of prayer and meditation followed by trying to compose my thoughts on paper.

The first few months didn't produce much of any substance, but I didn't give up. Slowly, God helped me to begin to really express myself. Writing began to be fun. The words started to flow. At first I wrote only about Shirley, and the pain of her loss, but gradually, I found myself writing about all kinds of things.

I remember one day, I had just sat down in the morning after prayer time, and started writing about everything I saw around me that was beautiful. Nothing missed my attention.

That night, some friends from church stopped by to check on me. My computer was on the table where we were sitting having a drink of iced tea. The screen was tilted toward my friend's wife, and she asked about it. After telling her and her husband about the journals, she asked if it was okay if she read it.

After finishing it, she told her husband he should read it too. I was deeply touched when she told me it had made her see the day we had just lived in a completely different way. She sort of embarrassed me the way she just kept gushing over it.

As they were leaving, I remember her taking my hand, and telling me I ought to consider writing a book. Although I didn't realize it then, I believe *Musings of a Walmart Greeter* was born that night.

Over the next few months, I prayed to God about what had been said to me that night. After several weeks, a theme began to emerge. "Everybody has a story," kept buzzing around in my head.

It all sort of came together one day while I was shopping at Walmart. As I was checking out, I looked around, and saw this melting pot of humanity all around me, and it was like a lightning bolt hit me standing there!

The whole world shops at Walmart! "If I am standing at the door of Walmart, I will get to watch the world pass me by!"

In the weeks and months after that day, a sort of restlessness settled over me. I couldn't get all those people and their stories out of my mind. I have coffee with a good friend once or twice a week, and I told him I was thinking about applying for a job as greeter at Walmart.

He sputtered, and nearly spilled his coffee! "You can't stand on that concrete all day!!" He was concerned that I would get bored. He knew my history, and he thought it might be a waste of my talents. He was not sure I could take orders from others! "Garry, you are not young anymore!"

Yep! He was pretty much right on all counts! It didn't make much sense, but those thoughts were swimming around in my head, and they wouldn't let go.

When that happens in my life, I have learned to let it go, and turn it over to God to guide me. It is a discipline that I learned from my first wife. Shirley was a deeply spiritual person, who talked to God all the time.

I am a "take charge, down the torpedoes" type of person, and she saw how critical it was in my daily walk that I had a shield to protect me from myself. God was my shield.

I began to pray very specifically every day about those thoughts swimming in my subconscious mind.

"Does every person's story matter?" "Is it any of my business?" "Lord, I am already busy in my daily life. There's church. There's Kiwanis! There's my family and friends! I enjoy just goofing off! Lord, I'm in my seventies!" I was a young man then (smile)!

I would pray those prayers every day. I have learned that God doesn't always send down His answers like a lightning bolt, although he can, and sometimes, does. For me, when I am truly patient, and empty my mind of MY preferences and leanings, and just become an empty vessel, waiting for God's answers, God never lets me down!

He takes His promises seriously! "I am with you till the end of time!"

The first time when I knew He was speaking to me was when this thought just popped into my mind. "Garry, don't you know that I have a story too! You are a part of My story. All of My creation is part of MY story."

The next signal came when I was reading my Bible one day, and I was in the book of Exodus. As I was reading, I heard this inner voice saying, "Moses was eighty when I sent him to lead My people out of Egypt! You are a young man, Garry!" I actually think I heard God chuckle at that last remark!

The final push came in church one Sunday. As I was listening to the sermon, I found my mind wandering, and when the answer came, I wasn't prepared, but I instantly knew God was speaking to me! "The world needs to hear My story! Look around you! Who isn't here! So many don't know Me! Don't be afraid! I am with you. Help others meet Me through stories about My children!"

I left church that morning KNOWING I had been in church! There were so many emotions surrounding me as I drove home. I remember just kneeling and praying when I got inside my apartment. I was scared, and excited, and humbled, and inspired. But I knew when I stood up that I was going to take action on God's answers!

Prayers continued. How would it happen? Where would I find the stories? How would I get people to talk? Would anybody even be interested in what I wrote?

Once again, I heard God's voice one day. "My son, wherever TWO are gathered in my name…if only one other person reads that book, it will be a success, because it will already have changed YOU!"

A few months later, I applied for a job at Walmart as a greeter, a position that is now referred to as a customer host. I was hired on October 27, 2016, and the exciting, and sometimes difficult, journey to this moment was begun.

From my very first day at the front door of Walmart, my antenna was up. Hundreds, sometimes thousands, of people poured through those doors every day. The first opportunity came in December when I connected with a WWII veteran when I was taking an electric cart from the grocery door to the general merchandise door. His story is the second chapter of this book, I still get choked up every time I read it.

There were lots of stops and starts. The "delete" button on my computer got over heated sometimes. It was an emotional roller coaster. Remember, this whole thing started out as a journal dealing with my beloved Shirley's death. There was the additional pressure of dealing with my promise to try to tell God's story too.

I remember one day when I had sat at my computer for almost three hours, and accomplished absolutely nothing! I had started several chapters, and deleted them all after a few sentences. They sucked! I deleted them all!

Finally, I decided to take a drive. I was just driving out in the middle of nowhere, and I remembered that I had not prayed for God's help one time that morning!

I pulled over beside the road, and bowed my head, and asked God to forgive me. He was my partner in this undertaking, and I hadn't even asked for his help.

All I can tell you is that the answer was immediate. The first thing I felt was an inner peace. The second thing I noticed was this sense of inspiration and energy to get busy. God is a GREAT partner!

I drove back to town and stopped by my friend's house for a cup of coffee. We celebrated the moment, and I returned home. I sat down at my computer, and the words flowed! In a little over two hours, another chapter was completed. Thank you, God!

There were many other challenges and bumps in the road as I pushed forward to get this thing finished. I lost both of my little Yorkies. Zoey died after bringing me joy and company for fifteen years. Tigger lived to the ripe old age of eighteen. That's about 126 years old in human years! I talk about them in the chapter about Wally.

I met my precious Nelia in late 2016 online, and we were married October 27, 2019. Her story is in another place in this book.

Nelia would suffer a major stroke on December 4, 2020, which would leave her unable to talk or walk, and almost totally paralyzed on her entire right side. After a valiant fight, she would die on November 1, 2021, from complications left by the stroke.

There have been thirteen surgeries. Two of them were life threatening. Seven of the thirteen surgeries occurred from June through October, just seven months after Nelia died. All but two were major surgeries. I had a PICC line port pumping strong antibiotics into my system to combat a potentially deadly infection that was ravaging my body. I remember one night laying in the hospital on the eve of my sixth surgery in four months. There were tubes and monitors everywhere. They were in the process of pumping twenty-one gallons of water in and out of my bladder, which was full of blood clots from internal bleeding. I had passed out at home from loss of blood that morning. I had been bleeding internally from complications from a catheter. Luckily, I had regained consciousness, and was able to call a friend who got me to the emergency room.

It had been a very long an depressing day. I was tired and weak from all the surgeries. I could have died if I hadn't been able to call my friend. It was 1:30 in the morning, and I was just ready to give up. Tears were rolling down my cheeks, and I remember squeezing my eyes shut, and whispering, "God, I can't take anymore! Please help me!"

Within minutes, I felt a quiet peace settle over me. God had answered my prayer! A nurse came into my room a few minutes later to check on me. I told her I was okay, and fell into a deep sleep as soon as she left. I didn't wake up until they came to take me to surgery. My depression had disappeared in the night. It has never returned.

During the past seven-and-a-half years, in addition to Nelia, I have lost my last sibling, my sister Pat, my sister in law, Betty, who I loved like a sister, a niece, a nephew, and two great nephews. Along the way, I have had to say "good bye" to a host of friends including a couple of high school buddies that had become encouragers and confidants over the years.

I'm in the fourth quarter of my life, so there have been some aches and pains I have had to deal with from time to time. One of the most challenging has been the arthritis in my hands. There have been times when Tylenol sat by my computer.

I have stopped and started so many times I have lost track. Three months ago, I was checking a customer's receipt when I felt light headed. When I came to my senses, I was half-in and half-out of the customer's shopping cart. People were scrambling to get me some help. I wasn't making much sense, but I managed to get control of myself.

There was no pain, but I thought I might be having a heart attack. Against everyone's advice, I drove myself home, and called my coffee buddy. He took me to the emergency room where I spent the next seven hours while the doctors were trying to figure out what had happened.

After an exhaustive examination and all kinds of tests, they determined that I had been "extremely fatigued and severely dehydrated." I could go home.

God had answered prayers again! During the seven hours I was in the hospital, my Facebook nearly blew up. Prayers had poured in from all over the world!

The next morning, there was a new energy and focus that had come over me during the night. That trip to the hospital could have ended differently. My mortality was staring me down. I knew that this book needed to be finished!

None of us know when we will take our final breath, but I had been sent a "wake up" call.

So here I am! So many have touched my life through these pages. The people I have met have sustained and transformed me. I am so grateful for my family doctor who got this all started. It's been an amazing journey! I have been blessed beyond words! Thanks for the ride!

Who knows? I'm only eighty-one! Maybe we will meet again! After all, everyone has a story!

Walmart Facts

- Sam Walton opened the first Walmart in Rogers, Arkansas July 2, 1992.
- By 1967, Walmart sales were up to $12.7 million.
- In 1968, Walmart opened its first store outside Arkansas in Sikeston, Missouri.
- In 1968, the company officially incorporated as Wal-Mart Stores, Inc.
- In 1970, Walmart became a publicly traded company. The first stock sold for $16.50 per share.
- In 1971, the first distribution center and home office opened in Bentonville, Arkansas.
- In 1972, Walmart is listed on the New York Stock Exchange (WMT) with fifty-one stores and sales of $78 million.
- In1975, inspired by a visit to a Korean manufacturing facility, Sam Walton introduces the Walmart cheer.
- Walmart's first pharmacy opened in 1978.
- In 1979, the Walmart Foundation is established.
- In 1980, Walmart sales reach $1 billion in annual sales for the first time. By now, there are 276 stores and 21,000 associates.
- In 1983, the first Sam's Club opens in Midwest City, Oklahoma. Walmart replaces cash registers with computerized point of sale systems, enabling fast and accurate checkout.
- In 1987, the Walton family establishes the Walton Family Foundation. The company installs the largest satellite communication system in the U.S., linking the company's operations through voice, data, and video communication.
- The first Walmart Supercenter opens in Washington, Missouri in 1988, combining general merchandise and a a full scale supermarket to provide one stop shopping convenience.
- In 1991, Walmart goes global, opening a Sam's Club in Mexico City.
- In 1992, Sam Walton receives the Medal of Freedom, shortly before passing away at age seventy-four. Rob Walton becomes chairman

of the board. By now, Walmart has 1928 stores and clubs, and employs 371,000 associates.
- In 1993, Walmart has its first $1 billion sales week!
- In 1994, Walmart expands into Canada with the purchase of 122 Woolco stores.
- In 1996, Walmart opens its first stores in China.
- In 1997, Walmart celebrates its first $100 billion year,
- In 1998, Walmart introduces the Neighborhood Market format in Bentonville, Arkansas. Walmart enters the United Kingdom with the acquisition of Asda.
- Walmart.com is founded in 2000, allowing U.S. Customers to shop online. There are 3,989 stores and clubs employing 1.1 million associates.
- In 2002, Walmart tops the Fortune 500 ranking of America's largest companies. Walmart purchases Seiyu, and enters the Japanese market.
- In 2006, Walmart introduces its $4 generic drug prescription program.
- In 2009, Walmart enters Chile. Walmart sales exceed $400 billion.
- In 2010, Bharti Walmart opens in India. Walmart commits $2 billion through the end of 2015 to end hunger in the United States, and launches a global commitment to sustainable agriculture, aiming to strengthen local farmers and economies, while providing customers access to affordable, high quality food.
- In 2011, Walmart expands into South Africa. Walmart surpasses 11,000 retail units around the world.
- In 2012, Walmart celebrates fifty years of helping people save money so they can live better.
- In 2013, Walmart announces it will hire any veteran within their first year off active duty. Walmart commits to buying $250 Billion in goods manufactured in the United States over the next 10 years.
- In 2014, Doug McMillon becomes CEO.
- In 2015, Walmart employs 2.3 million associates worldwide, and serves more than 200 million customers each week at more than 11,000 stores in 27 countries. Rob Walton retires as chairman of the board, and Greg Penner succeeds him.

- In 2017, Walmart launches free two-day shipping on more than 2 million items with no membership required.
- In 2018, the company changes its name from Wal-Mart Stores, Inc. to Walmart Inc.
- In 2019, Walmart launches InHome Delivery and free NextDay Delivery from Walmart.com.
- In 2021, Walmart invests in drone delivery, fintech, and autonomous vehicles. Walmart launches GoLocal last mile delivery sevrice.

More Interesting Walmart Facts
- The Walmart family still owns 50% of the company.
- Walmart has been the largest company in the world since 2001
- About 140 million customers visit Walmart stores or online every week.
- Walmart sells about 75 million products.
- A typical Walmart Superstore sells about 120,000 items of various categories.
- Bananas are the top selling Walmart product, topping over 1.5 billion pounds per year.
- Walmart sells about 330 million rolls of toilet paper every 3 week.
- Walmart's market share of American retail is 9.5%.
- Walmart services about 37 million customers every day.
- In 2022, the Walmart Foundation provided over $1.5 billion in cash and in-kind donations to support various initiatives.
- Walmart sources its products from more than one hundred countries.
- One of Walmart's key expansion plans is in the healthcare industry. Walmart has opened several healthcare clinics, which offer primary care, dental care, and mental health services. Walmart is also exploring the possibility of offering health insurance to its customers.
- Almost all Americans live within ten minutes of a Walmart store.
- Groceries are 55.7% of total sales.
- 75% of store managers started as hourly associates.

About the Author

Garry Warner was born in Syracuse, Kansas in 1943, and grew up on his parent's family farm in southwest Kearny County, Kansas. After graduating from Syracuse High School, he attended Bethany College in Lindsborg, Kansas and Kansas State Teachers College (now Emporia State University) in Emporia, Kansas, where he majored in Music Education.

Most of his adult life was spent in the automobile business in Wichita, Kansas, Omaha, Nebraska, St. Louis, Missouri, and finally in Sikeston, Missouri. He was a minority partner in Warner Pontiac, Oldsmobile, GMC in St. Louis. He served on Pontiac and GMC zone dealer councils, and the GMC National Dealers Council.

He and his first wife, Shirley moved to Sikeston, Missouri in 1992, where they owned and operated Premier Motor Company until her death in 2010. In 2019, he married Nelia Regala from the Philippines. She died in 2021.

He has been a member of Kiwanis International since 1989 and is a past governor of the Missouri Arkansas District and a past International Trustee.

He has been a member of First United Methodist Church since 1992.

He has worked for Walmart Store Number 9 in Sikeston as a greeter/customer host since 2016.

INDEX

B
Bentonville, Arkansas 27, 102, 148, 149
Branson, Missouri 102
Bryant, Dr. Cully 6
Byrd, Daniel 7

C
Caruthersville, Missouri 26, 27
Charleston, Missouri 116

D
Davis, Grant 20

H
Houston, Texas 103

K
Kansas City, Missouri 41
Kearny County, Kansas 12
Kennett, Missouri 27

L
Lindsborg, Kansas 13

M
Martinie, Mike 19
McFaddon, Chuck 17, 18
McFaddon, Jerry 18
McMillon, Doug 149
Memphis, Tennessee 27, 28
Midwest City, Oklahoma 148
Morris Township, New Jersey 71

O
Omaha, Nebraska 20, 151
Osburne, Bob 19

P
Penner, Greg 149

R
Reagan, Sam 20
Rogers, Arkansas 125, 137, 148
Rosenthal, Joe 24

S
Scarlett, Andrea 99, 100
Sikeston, Missouri 21, 26, 48, 63, 90, 122, 125, 126, 127, 137, 148, 151
St. Louis, Missouri 20, 21, 27, 45, 102, 103, 151
St. Peters, Missouri 21
Syracuse, Kansas 17, 18, 151

T
The Seeing Eye, Inc. 71, 72

U
Ulysses, Kansas 84
USS Arizona 22

V
Vietnam War 15

W
Walton, James "Bud" 137
Walton, Rob 148, 149
Walton, Sam 26, 27, 28, 41, 125, 126, 137, 148
Warner, Garry 6, 151
Warner, Larry 16, 17, 18, 19, 84, 135
Warner, Leroy (Buddy) 18, 135
Warner, Nelia 7, 21, 78, 79, 100, 101, 102, 103, 123, 127, 145, 151
Warner, Patty 18, 135
Warner, Shirley 6, 21, 85, 86, 95, 96, 103, 144, 151
Washington, Missouri 148
Watkins, Louis 6
Wichita, Kansas 16, 20, 151
World War II 22, 23, 24, 115, 116